JURORS'
RIGHTS

JURORS' RIGHTS

Jacqueline D. Stanley
Attorney at Law

Sphinx® Publishing
A Division of Sourcebooks, Inc.
Naperville, IL • Clearwater, FL

Second edition, 1998
    Published by: **Sphinx® Publishing: a division of Sourcebooks, Inc.®**

Naperville Office	Clearwater Office
P.O. Box 372	P.O. Box 25
Naperville, Illinois 60566	Clearwater, Florida 33757
(630) 961-3900	(813) 587-0999
FAX: 630-961-2168	FAX: 813-586-5088

Interior Design and Production: Shannon E. Harrington, Sourcebooks, Inc.

This publication is designed to provide accurate and authoritative information in regard to the subject matter covered. It is sold with the understanding that the publisher is not engaged in rendering legal, accounting, or other professional service. If legal advice or other expert assistance is required, the services of a competent professional person should be sought.
From a Declaration of Principles Jointly Adopted by a Committee of the American Bar Association and a Committee of Publishers and Associations

Library of Congress Cataloging-in-Publication Data

Stanley, Jacqueline D.
    Jurors' Rights / Jacqueline D. Stanley—2nd ed.
        p.   cm.
    Includes index.
    ISBN 1-57071-333-2 (pbk.)
    1. Jurors—United States—Popular works. 2. Jury duty—United States—Popular works.   I. Title.
KF8972.Z9S73 1998
347.73'752—dc21   97-52327
                                                                   CIP

Printed and bound in the United States of America.

Paperback — 10 9 8 7 6 5 4 3 2

CONTENTS

INTRODUCTION

Our modern jury system has come a long way. Historically, juries were convened for a variety of reasons. In 1879, a jury of matrons was summoned to decide whether a woman who was condemned to death was pregnant. This practice was condoned by the United States Supreme Court because it didn't want an innocent child to suffer the consequences of the mother's actions.

The role of the modern-day jury has evolved. Today, the jury's primary purpose is to decide guilt or innocence in criminal cases, and ascertain fault and assess damages in civil cases. Moreover, modern day jurors cannot be penalized for their decisions. However, that was not always the case. There was a time when the town council, believing a jury had reached a wrong decision, would convene another jury to decide if the first jury was guilty of bearing false witness against the accused. If the jury was found guilty, its punishment involved the loss of certain freedoms and property.

The jury is the foundation of a democratic legal system, a fact that has been true since the trial of Socrates—which was presided over by 500 of his peers—and most would agree that it is still true today. What people cannot agree on is the genesis of the jury system, although most historians would agree that the first jury trial was held in England sometime in 1351.

Unfortunately, today jurors are the unsung heroes of the legal system. They are drafted into service. They leave their jobs and families and go into the courtroom to protect the integrity of the legal system. Unlike the other participants in the trial process, they have no financial interest in the outcome. Unlike the lawyers, judges, and other court personnel, they don't rely on the legal system for their livelihood. Yet, criticism about the fairness of the judicial system tends to fall at the feet of the men and women who serve on the jury. Jurors have been lambasted for being ineffective and ignorant about what's going on around them. There have been loud cries for the revamping of the legal system and the creation of a professional juror pool or the elimination of juries altogether.

A jury of common citizens places a check on the judicial system to ensure that we remain a nation of laws and not of men. Jury duty allows regular people to get close up and personal with one of the most powerful institutions in our society. The integrity of our system separates us from many other countries and is a large part of what makes this country great. It is the responsibility of citizens to ensure the integrity of the system.

Can you imagine a system in which you could be brought before a judge, tried and convicted without ever knowing the charges against you or the identity of your accusers or prosecutors? If you have lived in America all your life, it is difficult to imagine such a system could exist anywhere other than in a Kafka novel. But the things we take for granted can be easily lost. It is the responsibility of each of us, as citizens, to serve as watchkeepers over our own fate. Serving on a jury provides this opportunity.

It also provides the opportunity to renew our faith in the justice system. Jury decisions in such high-profile cases as the trials of O.J. Simpson, the Menendez brothers, and the police officers accused of beating Rodney King are often criticized and threaten to erode the faith many people have in the jury system. Fortunately, there is hope. A 1992 study reported in the *Southern Methodist University Law Review* revealed that people who serve as jurors tend to have a greater appreciation and more positive attitude about the legal system than people who have never served on a jury.

During trials there is much said about the defendant's rights and the discussion of rights of victims is growing. However, the air falls silent on any discussions about the rights of the large group of civilian citizens summoned to participate in the legal system. Jurors are thrust into the system and saddled with the incredible responsibility of deciding the fate of a complete stranger. Regardless of how they decide, their decisions will be scrutinized, criticized, and second-guessed. The sacrifices they make to serve as jurors often go unappreciated and unacknowledged.

One common complaint of people who perform jury duty is that the defendant, in many instances, is treated better than the members of the jury. But, jurors should not be made to feel like victims of the system. They have rights, although there are many who believe jurors should not be informed of their rights. Fortunately, there are many others who share the belief that an informed juror is a good juror. This book was designed to perform that task and inform you of your rights and responsibilities as a juror.

Since the rights of jurors vary from state to state and often from county to county, this discussion will be general in scope. But it is guaranteed that you will be better informed after reading it than you were before you opened the book. It is hoped that the next time or the first time you open your mailbox and see your notification of jury duty, you will not feel imposed upon but rather feel honored that you have been given the opportunity to serve your community and participate in your government.

The scandal associated with many jurors in the O.J. Simpson trial and the length of the jury's sequestration have made jury duty appear about as attractive as an IRS audit or a trip to the dentist's office. Unlike no other case in history, the Simpson trial brought the legal system into the spotlight. Unfortunately, not all of what we saw was good. However, just as Simpson was an unusual defendant, so were the circumstances of the jury service unusual. It is neither logical nor fair to judge anything by its worst example. Life is ninety-nine percent attitude. The same is true of jury service. If you look at it as an opportunity instead of an inconvenience, the experience might be one you can look back on fondly as a learning experience.

> **Notes:** Sprinkled throughout this book are boxed notes like this one. They include facts and information about juries and jury service that, it is hoped, you will find both informative and entertaining.

THE RIGHT TO SERVE 1

Jury service has not been held to be a fundamental right. It is a privilege of citizenship. However, the absence of the right to serve on a jury must be considered in context with the jury's purpose, which is to benefit the litigants, not persons seeking to serve as jurors.

However, people can not be arbitrarily denied the opportunity of being selected as potential jurors. We each have a right not to be systematically excluded from the jury pool, which consists of the names of individuals randomly summoned to appear in court so it can be determined whether they are qualified to serve on a jury.

The Jury Selection and Service Act[1] prohibits discrimination in jury service on the basis or race, color, religion, sex, national origin, or economic status. This means potential jurors who have been systematically excluded from jury service may seek affirmative relief. The Jury Selection and Service Act also mandates that voting rolls be used to devise jury panels, not to allow federal jury commissioners to make lists autonomously.

The names of potential jurors are drawn from lists of voters. If the lists are not comprehensive enough to draw from a fair cross section of the community, other sources, such as driver's license registrations, must be tapped. The names must be selected randomly and the master list must be updated every four years.

It is conceivable that we may never be called to jury duty and someone else may be called several times. It is possible that the person who is summoned only once actually sits on a jury, while the person who is called several times never does. Jury service can be viewed like a state lottery. The state must allow everyone a fair opportunity to purchase a ticket, but not everyone has a right to win the jackpot.

Every juror who is summoned does not get to serve because potential jurors must be deemed competent to do so. Potential jurors have no input as to whether they will be selected to serve. The trial judge has the authority to decide whether a juror is competent to proceed. The judge must follow the guidelines set up by the state legislature as to who is and who is not qualified to serve on a jury. Unless the defendant in a criminal case is prejudiced by the judge's discretion, the defendant can not question the judge's authority. Potential jurors can't complain unless they are being discriminated against on the basis of their race, color, religion, sex, national origin, or economic status.

Each state decides its qualifications for jury service. Ordinarily, a potential juror must meet basic qualifications to serve:

1. They must be a citizen of the United States;

2. They must be a resident of the county where the case is being tried (the jury is supposed to reflect the ideas and attitudes of the community where it serves); and

3. They must meet a minimum-age requirement that generally ranges between eighteen and twenty-five.

What is the difference between a grand jury and a petit jury?

Grand juries are convened to determine whether there are sufficient facts and evidence to warrant a trial of the person accused. They are called grand juries because, usually, twenty-three jurors are impaneled. Petit juries are convened to decide questions of fact in civil and criminal cases and to reach a decision in conjunction with those findings. Ordinarily, they are composed of twelve members.

There is a myriad of things that might disqualify a person from jury service, or that are legitimate grounds for excusing a juror from service. These reasons for disqualification include the following:

1. *A prior felony conviction.* It is an unwritten rule that jurors should possess good moral character. It is also believed that felons are inherently biased against the legal system and the prosecution in criminal cases and will use jury service as an opportunity to express their resentment against the judicial system. A conviction of a minor crime or a conviction in another state might not disqualify a juror, and a potential juror who has received a pardon might be allowed to serve.

2. ***Deafness or blindness.*** One concern associated with deaf jurors would be the admission of a thirteenth person, the interpreter, into the jury deliberation room—a place that is considered off limits to everyone other than the six or twelve men and women selected to serve on the jury. Some states have specific laws that prohibit deaf persons from serving on a jury. Other jurisdictions, including the federal court system, leave it within the discretion of the trial judge. California, for example, at one time had a statute that automatically excluded blind or deaf jurors. The statute has been amended to allow handicapped jurors to serve. Many other jurisdictions require a rational basis for excluding jurors. It is important to note that the criminal defendant's right to a fair trial will, in most instances, pre-empt the potential juror's rights.

3. ***The inability to read or write.*** The question of written jury instructions creates the dilemma of what to do with jurors who cannot read or have difficulty reading. Illiteracy is considered an appropriate reason for dismissing potential jurors. Challenges to statutes that require potential jurors to be able to read English have been unsuccessful.

4. ***Refusal to take an oath, promise, or declaration to tell the truth.*** Historically, atheists were not allowed to serve as jurors. It was believed that people who did not believe in God had no fear of ramifications for telling lies. Today, juror oaths need not contain references to God. But, juror oaths that include references to God have been held by the courts not to violate the United States Constitution's prohibitions

against the enactment of laws respecting "the establishment of religion."

In one case a juror refused to take an oath that contained the phrase "so help me God" or to take an affirmation that contained no reference to God. The trial judge held her in civil contempt.[2] The juror filed a civil rights action against the judge, arguing that the judge's actions infringed upon her free exercise of religion. The appellate court eventually ruled in her favor, deciding that her claims involved both her right to free speech and the free exercise of religion. The court found that she should be allowed to make a promise or declaration to tell the truth. The court suggested that in some instances jurors should be allowed to draft their own statements or commitments to tell the truth.

5. *Disloyalty, to the United States.* A person who expresses a disloyalty to the United States government. An expression of disloyalty would rarely be a factor except in criminal cases. It will only apply in civil cases in which the government is a party in the case.

6. *A mental or physical defect.* The defect must make the juror incapable of fulfilling his or her duties. The infirmity must exist at the time of service, and disqualification can't be solely based on a defect that only existed in the past.

7. *Inability to understand the English language.* Potential jurors must be able to speak and understand the English language to the extent that they can participate in the deliberations and understand what is being said in the proceedings.

REASONS QUALIFIED JURORS ARE EXCUSED

While the above reasons would disqualify a potential juror, the following list includes reasons why otherwise qualified jurors are likely to be excused from service:

1. Attitude. The potential juror has formulated a specific attitude with respect to the nature of the case or the possible result.

2. Empathy. The potential juror appears to empathize with a party, the victim, or the victim's family.

3. The potential juror has a vested interest in a similar case. For example, he once sued a bank for the same reason the plaintiff is now suing a bank.

4. The potential juror once served as a witness or juror in a case similar to the case being tried. There is a fear that the juror might apply his or her past experiences to the present case.

5. The potential juror served as a juror or witness, or somehow participated in the trial of the defendant in another or similar matter.

6. The potential juror has bet on how the case will be resolved.

7. The potential juror is in a unique position to have previous knowledge of the case. For example, she or he has an intimate relationship with someone who investigated the claims against the defendant.

8. The potential juror is racially or sexually biased.

9. The potential juror is prejudiced against witnesses in the case.

10. The potential juror is biased in favor of law enforcement. People who are related to law enforcement personnel are routinely excused from jury duty in criminal cases.

11. The potential juror doesn't believe in capital punishment or other possible punishments. A person who says they don't believe in and would not vote to have someone executed would not be allowed to serve on a jury in a capital murder case.

12. The potential juror has strong feelings about certain crimes. They or their loved ones might have been victims of that type of crime.

13. The potential juror has strong feelings about certain defenses.

14. The potential juror has strong feelings about certain types of lawsuits.

15. The potential juror is related to someone connected with the trial—a party, a witness, or anyone that might make them favor one side over the other.

16. The potential juror has a business relationship with a party, a witness, or anyone involved in the trial that might make them favor one side over the other.

Voir Dire

The court is able to determine whether a juror is competent through a procedure known as *voir dire* (a French word, pronounced "vwa deer," which literally means "to speak the truth"). Voir dire is the examination or questioning of jurors to determine their fitness to hear a particular case. The purpose of the voir dire is to provide the judge and the attorneys on both sides with sufficient information to determine if potential jurors can be fair or if they possess any possible biases or prejudices.

Jurors can be questioned on matters that will provide the court and the attorneys with insight on the prospective juror's bias or prejudice. However, voir dire should not be used to deny people the opportunity to serve on a jury.

There are three methods of voir dire:

1. Federal method. In federal court the judge conducts the examination and asks the questions. The attorneys on each side are allowed to submit suggested questions to the judge.

2. State method. Both the judge and the attorneys conduct the examination and ask the questions.

3. Alternate state method. The attorneys conduct the examination and ask the questions.

In criminal cases in which the attorneys are allowed to question the jury, they often employ jury consultants, psychological rating scales, surveys, and questionnaires to help them with jury selection.

The court will sometimes limit the number of questions, regardless of who conducts the examination, but the questioning can get very intense. Prospective jurors are not on trial, however. And despite proclamations to the contrary, lawyers do not want an impartial jury. They want a jury that is favorable to their position. Lawyers might excuse a person from jury service because of the person's impartiality.

During voir dire, each attorney will be given a specific number of *peremptory challenges*, which allow parties to excuse an otherwise qualified juror without explanation, and without scrutiny by the judge. In criminal cases, the defense will be given more peremptory challenges than the prosecution.

Peremptory challenges can be used to exclude jurors with a specific bias. They can not be used to exclude "group bias" by excluding segments of society like African Americans or, women or Catholics. Consequently, there are restrictions placed on the type of questions permitted during voir dire.

An otherwise competent prospective juror can not be disqualified because of religious beliefs or status, and the mere potential for bias based on religious affiliation cannot justify the exclusion of a prospective juror.

Questions about a juror's religious beliefs are proper on voir dire when religious issues are presently and expressly involved in the case, or when a religious organization is a party to the litigation. Questioning jurors about their religious beliefs has been allowed in cases dealing with abortion, polygamy, and selective service laws. In other instances, however, inquiries into a potential juror's religious beliefs or affiliations are inappropriate, particularly when there are no religious issues in the case. Generally, questions relating to jurors' religious beliefs are inadmissible in civil cases.

CASE STUDIES

- In a case where the defendant pleaded insanity and claimed God told him to commit murder, the defense attorney appealed the jury's guilty verdict on the basis that he was not allowed to inquire on voir dire about the jurors' potential religious bias. The conviction was affirmed.[3]

- In another instance, a man convicted of burglarizing a Catholic rectory and robbing and assaulting two Catholic priests appealed on the basis that he was not allowed to exclude all Catholics from serving on the jury. His conviction was also upheld.[4] In another case, a man convicted of assault could not exclude a prospective juror because he attended the same church as an associate of the prosecuting attorney.[5]

OBJECTIONABLE QUESTIONS

Questions regarding religious beliefs or affiliations are not the only type of questions many juror's consider objectionable. However, there is a right way and a wrong way for jurors to express their objection to questions. A California case illustrates how potential jurors should not respond when faced with objectionable questions. In the case a judge held a prospective juror in contempt and sentenced her to a day in jail for refusing to answer questions about her marital status during the voir dire examination. The woman complained that only the women had been asked that question and a question about their spouses' occupations. She alleged the questioning constituted sex discrimination. She argued that if everyone had been asked these questions she would have quickly responded. The California appellate court held that she was justified in refusing to answer the question. But, the court found she should have used a nonconfrontational method to state her objection, such as writing a letter of complaint to the judge. The lesson here is that jurors should use non-aggressive means in asserting their rights.[6]

The most effective means of responding to an objectionable question is to turn to the judge and explain the specific nature of the objection.

EXEMPTIONS

Qualified jurors are often allowed to avoid jury duty because they are exempt. Each state legislature determines who is exempt from jury service. In many states, certain professions are exempt from jury service. These professions include:

1. Police and other law enforcement personnel.

2. Fire department personnel.

3. Doctors and dentists.

4. School teachers who are active during the school term.

5. People with custody of their minor children under twelve years old.

6. Telephone and telegraph operators.

7. Rescue and ambulance personnel.

8. Court personnel.

Federal court rules allow the following exemptions:

1. People over seventy years old.

2. Active ministers.

3. People with custody of their minor children under twelve years old.

4 Lawyers and law students.

5. Doctors, dentists, and nurses.

There is no such thing as a permanent exemption. Although you might be in an exempted class, you will still be in the jury pool and might be periodically summoned for jury duty. Judge Lance Ito was summoned to jury duty during the O.J. Simpson trial.

An exemption gives a prospective juror the opportunity to decline to serve, but it doesn't mean that a prospective juror is disqualified from serving. And although a person might be a member of an exempted class, he or she can still conceivably serve on a jury assuming they survive voir dire.

A prospective juror should establish their exempt status during or before voir dire. For example, a doctor who doesn't claim his exemption during or before voir dire, cannot subsequently be excused because he is a doctor. He might, however, be excused on other grounds.

HARDSHIP CASES

A juror might be excused if serving would cause him or her a *severe hardship*, such as:

1. The juror lives a long distance from the courthouse and doesn't have reliable transportation.

2. The juror needs to work to support his or her family.

3. The juror has health problems.

4. The juror has family problems that need his or her immediate attention.

5. The juror has previous commitments, such as a trip around the world that is already paid for and scheduled to depart the day the trial is scheduled to begin.

6. The juror has personal or business affairs that require immediate attention.

7. The juror has physical or emotional problems.

8. The juror must attend to another case in which he or she is a party or witness.

Prior to the return of the verdict, if both sides agree, federal rules allow a jury of fewer than twelve persons to hear a criminal case. This would become necessary when a juror needs to withdraw because of illness or some extreme hardship, and the alternate jury pool has been depleted.

Once you are selected to serve on a jury, absent a showing of misconduct, you cannot be excused from service unless it is shown that continuing service would create undue hardship or is extremely inconvenient.

MISCONDUCT

The primary reason jurors are excused after being selected is misconduct. Courts are more stringent about misconduct in criminal cases than in civil cases. Juror misconduct is determined on a case-by-case basis. It can occur inside and outside the jury room. Since what happens in the jury room is secret, most of the conduct there goes undetected. When it is detected, it is difficult to prove because most of what is said in jury deliberations is inadmissible in subsequent proceedings. Thus, juror misconduct generally has to be proven by evidence from persons other than the jurors. In order to justify a mistrial and the granting of a new trial on the basis of juror misconduct, the complaining party generally has to show that he has been prejudiced as a result of the misconduct.

EXAMPLES OF JUROR MISCONDUCT

1. Conducting an independent investigation or consulting an independent source outside the jury room, and bringing that information into the deliberations.

2. Reading about the case in the newspaper or watching a television news program that covers the case, and using that information in deliberations.

3. Discussing the case with people not on the jury.

4. Discussing the existence of insurance coverage in a civil case when that information was not introduced as evidence.

5. Drawing lots or flipping coins to decide a case.

6. Visiting the scene of the accident or crime that is the subject of the trial.

7. Having contacts with any of the parties of the case or with an attorney for any party.

8. Taking a nap during the trial or being inattentive.

9. Drinking alcohol or using illegal narcotics during the course of the trial.

CASE STUDIES OF JUROR MISCONDUCT

- In one case, a juror received a ride from the plaintiff to and from the trial. The court found this to be misconduct, although the two did not discuss the case.[7]

- In an arson and manslaughter case, a juror rode home with firefighters who had been witnesses for the prosecution. Although the parties did not discuss the case, the court described the misconduct as "inexcusable and reprehensible" and ordered that the defendant be given a new trial.[8]

- In a murder case, a prosecution witness told an alternate juror that the defendant was guilty of murdering other people in addition to the person he was charged with killing. Three jurors overheard the alternate juror relaying this information to a third party. The court decided this conduct warranted a mistrial.[9]

- In one case, the bailiff, who was related to one of the defendants, introduced his family to the jury. He told the jurors not to allow a specific individual to be the foreman. He also told one of the jurors that he would tell her husband if she did a bad job, and told the jurors he would contact them after the trial because he was running for political office. The court considered this conduct improper.[10]

• It was found to be misconduct when the jury foreman in a murder case asked an attorney not connected with the case for an explanation of manslaughter.[11]

THIRD-PARTY COMMUNICATIONS

Communication between jurors and third parties is the most common form of misconduct. But not all such communication will be deemed misconduct. Misconduct involving jurors and third parties is based on the following factors:

1. The nature of the communications.

2. Where the conversation took place.

3. Who initiated the conversation.

4. The intent of the conversation.

5. Whether the conversation influenced the juror.

6. How the juror reacted to the conversation.

7. What interest the third party had in the case.

8. The number of jurors involved in the communication.

IS THERE A RIGHT NOT TO SERVE?

Can you elect not to serve on a jury by ignoring the summons, or by appearing in court and refusing to answer questions? No.

Failing to respond to a summons in most states carries a fine and in some instances a jail sentence. If there is a legitimate emergency or reason for not appearing in court, you can call a phone number that is usually included on the summons and explain your situation. Refusing to answer questions or providing false answers can result in your being held in contempt of court, which could also mean a fine or jail sentence.

The most sound course of action is to appear in court and answer truthfully the questions presented, unless you feel strongly that they are discriminatory or an invasion of your privacy, in which case you should respectfully inform the judge of your feelings. The judge will then tell you whether you must answer. If the judge instructs you to answer the question, you should answer (unless, of course, you are prepared to go to jail, then hire a lawyer to file an appeal of your contempt of court citation and try to prove the question was improper).

The Lighter Side of Jury Duty

A murder trial, in which the jury had been sequestered, was finally winding up when one of the jurors began to suffer the effects of a severe toothache. Rather than dismiss the juror and allow an alternate juror to serve in his place, the judge ordered the juror to seek treatment. Because the judge had previously ordered the panel to remain together he ordered the other eleven jurors to accompany their fellow juror to the hospital emergency room's dental clinic.

— *National Law Journal*, March 26, 1984

THE RIGHT TO COMPENSATION 2

The adage that doing the right thing is its own reward is certainly applicable in the case of jury duty. Jurors can expect to be compensated for their service to their community. However, unless they work in a sweat shop staffed by illegal aliens, the compensation jurors receive won't come close to what they earn through their regular means of employment.

One unfortunate consequence of the paltry fees paid jurors and the fact that many jurisdictions no longer recognize financial hardship as an excuse from jury service is that only people at or below the poverty level can afford to serve on a jury. The low fees are also the reason people who earn a significant income avoid jury duty like a bad investment.

The Uniform Jury Service and Selection Act[1], a Federal law, mandates that jurors be paid according to a rate that is specifically established in the state statutes. Jurors are paid a daily rate for each day they are required to attend court, and they will be compensated even if they are not called to hear a case.

In North Carolina, for example, juror's are paid $12 per day. When a juror is required to serve for more than five days in any two-year period, they receive $30 for each day they serve in excess of five days. In California and New Jersey, jurors receive as little as $5 per day.

Members of the O.J. Simpson jury, who were sequestered for more than nine months, received only about $1,400 for their services, although it was reported that they were treated to performances by comedians, baseball games, and beach trips.

Jurors in Colorado, Connecticut, Massachusetts and Wyoming receive a much higher rate of compensation. The daily rate for jury duty in those jurisdictions is $50 per day. The difference in the daily pay rate for jurors across the country is based on many factors, including the following:

1. The state's fiscal health.

2. The state's median family income.

3. The generosity of the state legislature.

4. The value the legislature places on jury service.

The rate of compensation for serving on a federal jury is $40 per day. This rate applies throughout the federal circuit. Thus, federal jurors who sit in a North Carolina case will be paid the same rate as federal jurors who sit in a Nevada case.

There are many reasons juror compensation is so low and will probably remain that way. These reasons include:

1. The legislature does not want jury service to be considered employment, but rather a duty that citizens have the privilege of performing.

2. The fee is not intended to compensate jurors for their time but to offset minor expenses of service.

3. As money is considered by some misguided people to be the root of all evil, the absence of profit in jury service is believed to ensure that the people who assume the responsibility to serve on a jury will perform honestly.

4. Increasing the compensation might encourage jurors to extend their deliberations in order to inflate the fee they receive.

5. Millions of people serve on juries each year. Most states can barely afford to fill the potholes in the road; few can afford the expense associated with increasing the juror fee.

> Each year jurors in the U.S. receive $200 million in compensation. Jurors' absence from work costs employers nearly $1 billion annually.
>
> — *Time*, September 28, 1981

RELATED EXPENSES

Most state statutory schemes require jurors to be compensated for the following expenses associated with jury service:

1. Expenses for travel to and from the courthouse. The rate of pay for these expenses must be specifically designated in the statute. In some jurisdictions, jurors will only be

permitted mileage expenses if they are summoned to perform jury duty in a county outside where they reside.

2. In the event jurors are sequestered and required to remain overnight at the site of the trial, they are entitled to be furnished with adequate lodging and meals.

3. Jurors should be compensated for or provided meals if they are required to stay together as a group during the trial, although they are not sequestered.

EMPLOYER COMPENSATION AND LEAVE

A majority of states have laws that prohibit employers from firing employees who are summoned for jury duty. A few states also have laws that require employers to pay their employees for a certain period of time while they are serving on a jury, or that deduct the state juror pay if the employer voluntarily pays the employee for jury duty. Fortunately, many employers provide jury leave, although they are not required to do so. Most employee unions insist on including jury leave in employment contracts.

OUTSIDE SOURCES OF COMPENSATION

Jurors who receive the dubious honor of being selected to serve on high-profile cases such as the O.J. Simpson, Menendez brothers, or Susan Smith trials, are often presented with the opportunity to sell their stories after the trial. There were reports that O.J. Simpson trial jurors were offered and paid as much as $200,000 for interviews with the tabloids and talk shows. There were also reports of book deals with promises of even greater compensation.

One problem brought to light by the O.J. Simpson trial is that jurors might focus more on obtaining book contracts than getting to the heart of the trial. Several jurors were dismissed based on rumors that they were considering book contracts or keeping notes for books, and a few dismissed jurors showed up on talk and news shows such as *Good Morning America*.

However, despite the potential for problems, jurors usually are not prohibited from telling or selling their stories after they have been released from service. Judges may, in many instances, encourage jurors to keep their deliberations private, but judges usually don't issue a restraining order because of jurors' First Amendment right to free speech. If a restraining order is issued, jurors should contact an attorney before deciding to violate the order.

The Lighter Side of Jury Duty

After thirteen days of deliberations, a jury panel in a Brooklyn, New York, case began complaining about the food they were being served. The jurors told the judge they wanted foods fancier than the standard American fare. The judge ordered that they be treated to calzone or egg foo young.

— *National Trial Journal*, March 24, 1986

The Right to Privacy 3

People who have never been summoned to jury service or endured voir dire, or are not familiar with the legal system, might be surprised to learn that privacy is an important consideration to jurors, who are often asked to respond to fairly personal questions in front of a room of strangers.

Most jurors are perplexed about why their favorite television program or a question of where there children attend school is relevant to jury duty. Privacy is not an issue in every case and will often depend on the nature of the case.

Certainly, the questions jurors will be asked in a shoplifting case will not be nearly as sensitive or personal as the questions asked in a rape or other sex-related crime case. Moreover, some people are more sensitive than others, so privacy issues have to be considered on a case-by-case basis.

While jurors should expect their privacy to be encroached upon to some extent, entering the jury box does not mean jurors lose their right to privacy in matters where most reasonable people would expect to maintain privacy. The U.S. Supreme Court introduced the principle that an individual has a constitutionally protected right to refuse to disclose certain personal matters for which they have a reasonable expectation of privacy.[1]

Most judges will take measures to accommodate jurors expectation of privacy, realizing that if jurors expectations of privacy are not protected, jurors might be inclined to hide information, provide false information, or take measures to avoid jury service altogether. While judges might sometimes behave as if they know everything, they are not mind readers. The squeaking wheel gets the oil. If a juror has a concern about her privacy, she should convey it to the judge. Moreover, the polite wheel gets more oil than the rude wheel.

While the questioning might concern private matters, jurors should not take personal offense to what is being asked. The intent of voir dire is not to delve into a person's private affairs. When expressing concerns about privacy, jurors need not make a personal attack on the judge or attorney. Life inside the jury box will proceed a lot smoother if there is no hostility between jurors and the judge.

Pre-Trial Investigations

The invasion into a juror's privacy can begin before the trial does. Most potential jurors might not be aware that before the trial begins, they could be the subject of an investigation into their personal background. The purpose of pre-trial investigations is to detect impartial and biased jurors.

In federal cases, U.S. attorneys have ready access to official government files concerning prospective jurors. Defense attorneys, on the other hand, usually use private investigators to check into the backgrounds of potential jurors. Much to the chagrin of potential jurors, courts generally will not interfere with pre-trial investigations.

Things have come a long way in the area of pre-trial investigations. According to a report in a 1928 case, police had to personally endorse prospective jurors by investigating and reporting on prospective jurors' reputations, drinking habits, and morality.[2] And what happened in an 1958 case would send chills up the spine of any potential juror.[3]

In that case, a mobster was prosecuted for tax evasion. The district attorney's office requested an investigation into each prospective juror's tax return. The prosecution used the information to rate the jurors. Potential jurors with little or no contact with the IRS were given the highest ratings.

Investigators often check into a prospective juror's credit rating, family background, and reputation in their community. There have been reported instances in which photographers have been hired to photograph prospective jurors homes.

Investigators also peruse voter registration lists to ascertain jurors political party affiliations. They visit a county register of deeds office to try to find out whether jurors are homeowners or renters. They can also make legitimate guesses about jurors' incomes based on where jurors live, which is also a good indication of a juror's race. Investigators can also pull a juror's police record. A driver's license is filled with information that attorneys on both sides might consider useful. One defense attorney was quoted as saying, "A juror sits in judgment of other human beings, and it's terribly important to know everything you can about him."

Jurors will not be investigated in every case, however. Investigations are very expensive, and it's fortunate for potential jurors that most parties in litigation cannot afford these expenses, in addition to their legal fees. Unfortunately, in cases in which potential jurors are investigated, much or all of what is uncovered will remain a mystery to the juror who was investigated. In one instance, a juror unsuccessfully sued the state of California for $50,000 when the judge refused to order the parties to divulge to the juror the information uncovered about him.[4]

RELEASE OF POTENTIAL JURORS' NAMES, ADDRESSES, AND PHONE NUMBERS

The reason pre-trial investigations are possible is because potential jurors names, addresses, and phone numbers are considered public information and are released before the trial. Jury lists may remain confidential until the morning of the trial, but there is a federal statute that provides for releasing lists of jurors and witnesses at least three days before trial in cases involving treason and capital offenses. Otherwise, local federal rules decide when the list of information will be released. Most state statutes do not clearly outline the restrictions regarding juror information.

People who are new to the jury experience might not realize that their name, address, and phone number could be available, not only to the parties in the litigation, but to the public as well. Such information is available to anyone, including the media, so it is possible—but not likely in most cases—that this information could find its way into the local newspaper.

The media's access to jurors names and addresses must take the following considerations into account.

1. The defendant's Sixth Amendment right to a fair trial by an impartial jury. Public and media access to jurors names, phone numbers, and addresses is allowed, it is believed, to ensure that the defendant will be able to receive an impartial jury. There is an argument that suggests that if jurors realize they are not operating in a vacuum they will be more inclined to tell the truth on voir dire rather than risk being exposed, and the media might discover falsehoods that might not otherwise be uncovered.

2. The media's First Amendment right. It is believed that the news media are the public's eyes and ears, and that the media place an important check on the government. Thus, the media's First Amendment right to access to public information is firmly entrenched in our society.

3. The public's right to know. This consideration goes hand in hand with the media's First Amendment right. The public would soon become distrustful of a legal system in which jurors were able to sit in the jury box with paper bags over their heads and without having to reveal their identity.

4. The juror's right to privacy. Unfortunately, this right to privacy is not as firmly entrenched as the defendant's and the media's rights. Jurors' privacy rights are grounded in the principle of "a reasonable expectation of privacy." The reason the law does not provide more restrictions, and the reason lawsuits in this area are generally unsuccessful, is because it is difficult to formulate an argument that supports the claim that jurors have an expectation of privacy in their names, phone numbers, or addresses. Fortunately, there have been no reported cases where information about a juror was misused and a juror harmed by the release of information.

QUESTIONING ABOUT PRIVATE AFFAIRS

The Supreme Court has recognized a defendant's right during voir dire to make peremptory challenges in the attempt to select an impartial jury.[5] This means the Supreme Court has given defendants broad latitude in examining jurors. This examination of the jurors can often tread into areas that jurors might find delicate and sensitive. Rape cases, in particular, often include questions of a sexual nature.

A juror's right to privacy usually gives way to the defendant's Sixth Amendment rights because personal information about the jurors that is relevant to the case must be disclosed during voir dire. However, during a murder case when one prospective juror refused to answer twenty questions on the 110 question questionnaire regarding her personal habits and her favorite television programs, her contempt citation was set aside by an appellate court on the basis that it violated her 14th Amendment right to privacy.[6]

Although potential jurors can appeal a judge's order that forces them to answer questions they consider private, it is important to note that the trial judge is given broad discretion when conducting and presiding over voir dire. Generally, questions about the following will be allowed:

1. Name

2. Address

3. Age

4. Marital and family status

5. Occupation of both the juror and their spouse

6. Dates of employment

7. Number of children

8. Children's school or occupation

9. Relationship to law enforcement personnel

10. Education or academic background

However, potential jurors should not hesitate to challenge the relevancy of the following list of questions:

1. Political affiliation

2. Religious affiliation or beliefs

3. Health

4. Sexual orientation, habits or experiences

5. Personal habits

6. Income

The judge, in most instances, will take measures to protect jurors' privacy during voir dire. Courts are afraid that the fear of interrogation will frighten people away from jury service. Moreover, they realize that jurors can refuse to answer a question if they feel their privacy interests outweigh the defendant's right or need to know. If a juror is forced to answer, they can appeal the order, and the trial may be delayed until the appellate court decides.

DENYING THE MEDIA AND PUBLIC ACCESS TO VOIR DIRE

The fact that voir dire is usually conducted in open court creates many of the privacy issues. One option the judge has is to close the doors of the courtroom to the media and other spectators. But, the court will only close the courtroom if the judge feels it is absolutely necessary.

The U.S. Supreme Court has identified public access to criminal proceedings as a constitutional right. Thus, before the trial court can order the closure of voir dire it must be able to establish the following:

1. Closure must be narrowly tailored to serve the interest it was intended to served. For instance, if one juror has expressed concern about his privacy it would be appropriate to close the courtroom while that juror is being examined. However, it would not be appropriate to close the

courtroom while the entire jury panel is being examined if none of the others have expressed any concern.

2. Closure must be the only viable option. The judge is expected to consider less restrictive measures before deciding to close the courtroom. Jurors should not hesitate to offer solutions for the court. Sometimes it might be appropriate to conduct voir dire inside the judge's chambers with only the court reporter, attorneys from both sides, and the judge present.

3. Closure must allow access to nonsensitive issues, so it is unusual for the entire voir dire process to be closed. Information such as jurors' names, addresses, and occupations will usually allow the courtroom to be open to the public.

4. The court must make specific findings as to why closure is necessary. The judge will have to prepare a written order that clearly outlines why the court has decided to close the courtroom, which is why potential jurors who request the courtroom closure should articulate their concerns as definitively and unemotionally as possible.

POST-TRIAL INTERVIEWS

There are three types of post-verdict interviews:

1. One or more of the attorneys in the litigation might try to interview jurors to obtain some feedback about the attorney's performance.

2. One or more of the attorneys might interview jurors to determine why they decided the case the way they did, in order to challenge the verdict or decision.

3. The media might interview jurors to get the behind-the-scenes story to share with the public.

The court's power to protect jurors from inspection by the press does not end with the verdict. Many jurors also consider post-verdict interviews to be an invasion of their privacy. Judges are permitted to prohibit attorneys from badgering jurors for interviews or about how they voted on the case. Lawyers generally need the judge's permission to contact the jurors. The trial judge often specifically informs lawyers not to contact jurors, unless they do so through the court. Usually, the interviews will be conducted in the presence of the judge.

Courts are split on whether they should allow post-verdict interviews. Many allow interviews by attorneys, however, eyebrows are quickly raised when members of the media conduct the interviews. Most federal rules regarding post-verdict interviews deal with lawyers, their agents, and the media. In one case the U.S. Supreme Court upheld the trial court's order enjoining nonparties (including the news media) from questioning jurors after the trial.[7]

The principle on which all courts are in agreement is that secrecy is the fundamental element of the deliberation process. Jurors are encouraged not to talk about their deliberations, and courts will generally bend over backwards to assist and support jurors who do not wish to be interviewed after a trial. They do so because they realize people will be more honest if they know what goes on behind jury doors will be forever private. One court held that, "If jurors are conscious that they will be subject to interrogation or searching hostile inquiry as to what occurred in the jury room and why, they are almost inescapably influenced to some extent by that anticipated annoyance."[8]

The Lighter Side of Jury Duty

Certain information can slip past even the most intrusive of voir dire examinations. A husband and wife were allowed to serve on the same jury panel in an Olmsted County, Minnesota case. The wife used her maiden name, and no one asked either party about their spouse's name.

— *National Trial Journal*, March 30, 1981

THE RIGHT TO SAFETY 4

Many have analogized that civilians are drafted into jury service in the same way civilians are drafted into military service. While we might expect military service could be hazardous to one's health, few people would expect the same to be true of jury service. However, as the world becomes increasingly violent, a courtroom is not necessarily a safe place to be any longer. Newspaper headlines have reported stories of crazed defendants going on shooting rampages in courtrooms.

Admittedly, these episodes are rare. What presents a more common problem for jurors are threats and harassment from parties in the litigation or people who are acting on their behalf in an attempt to persuade jurors to rule a certain way. There have been reported instances, particularly in high-profile cases, in which jurors have been threatened and injured by associates of the defendant. But, while jurors have from time to time been threatened, physical injury to a juror has been traced to a defendant in only one case.[1] In that case, the jury foreman received a back injury during the course of the trial, which was subsequently attributed to the defendant.

Fortunately, courts generally will take whatever steps are necessary to protect jurors and ensure that jurors feel safe. The courts realize that if jurors feel frightened or threatened during a trial, they may be unable to render an impartial verdict. The courts also realize that if the general public perceives jury duty as inherently unsafe, it will avoid jury service.

JURY TAMPERING

Discussions about juror safety are often associated with conversations about jury tampering. Jury tampering is the unauthorized contact or communication between a party involved in the litigation (or third parties) and members of the jury which is designed to influence the jury's decision. Jury tampering is considered a serious matter and can take many different forms not all of which are intended to threaten jurors safety. These forms of tampering include the following:

1. Harassing phone calls.

2. Threatening letters.

3. Physical assaults.

4. Monetary bribes.

5. Blackmail.

6. Stalking.

7. Damage to property.

8. Any other contact or communication not overseen by the court.

This list was not intended to be all inclusive. The U.S. Supreme Court has determined that "any unapproved private communication, contact or tampering with a juror during a criminal trial is presumptively prejudicial."[2] The Supreme Court has acknowledged that a defendant can't possibly have received a fair trial if the jurors are sitting in fear or are under influence from outside sources. However, the court's provision that unapproved contact or tampering is "presumptively" prejudicial opens the door for the trial court to exercise its discretion in deciding whether a particular contact is prejudicial.

CASE STUDIES IN JURY TAMPERING

- A federal court ruled that there was no prejudice when a juror's husband discussed the case with spectators as there was no finding that the juror had discussed anything with her husband.[3]

- In a case where a courtroom spectator stated that it would be too bad if the elevator filled with jurors crashed, a federal court decided that it was not prejudicial because it was found not to have influenced jurors as none of the jurors heard it.[4]

- In a case in which a juror was receiving threatening phone calls, the court held that there was no prejudice to the defendant since the juror believed that the threatening phone calls he received were from "prankish youngsters" and not the defendant.[5]

- The court held that there was no prejudice to the defendant in a case where several members of the jury received material with quotations from the Bible and the United States Constitution.[6]

- In a case in which the sheriff informed two jurors that the defendant "had done something like this before"—bludgeoning his victim to death with a pool cue—the court determined that the comment did prejudice the defendant as there had been no evidence of prior violent crimes by the defendant.[7]

The examples below illustrate the three factors courts consider when considering allegations of jury tampering. These are also things you should take into account when evaluating whether you have been the victim of jury tampering:

1. *Who is the source of the alleged tampering?* If the defendant or someone acting on their behalf is the person who initiates the contact or communication, it's more likely to be deemed tampering than if someone who is not related or only remotely connected to the case or its outcome does so.

2. *What influence did the alleged tampering have on the jury?* This factor brings to mind the question, if a tree falls in the forest and no one is there to hear it, does it make a sound? If the defendant launches a threat that jurors are not aware of or that they do not perceive as a threat, in most instances it will not be considered tampering.

3. *What is the nature of the alleged tampering?* Since tampering can take many forms, the form of the contact or communication is an important consideration. The more direct the

contact or communication, the more likely it will be deemed tampering. Although it's important to note that not all jury tampering need take the form of a threat to the jurors safety or well being, immediate threats to jurors will in most instances be deemed tampering.

If there is evidence of tampering, a hearing is held to determine the affect it has had on jurors and whether it would be prejudicial to either party to allow the juror to continue to serve. The court has several options when it does find evidence of jury tampering, including the following:

1. If the tampering is widespread or serious, the court can declare a mistrial. The person guilty of the unauthorized contact or communication can be forced to face criminal charges under any applicable statutes.

2. The court can discharge individual jurors who have been tampered with and allow alternative jurors to proceed in their place.

3. The court can find that while there might have been evidence of jury tampering, it was not to the extent that it would preclude the defendant from receiving a fair trial, and allow the case to proceed.

4. The court can take measures to preclude any additional tampering.

SEQUESTRATION

If there is a serious risk that jurors might be influenced by outside sources, they are sequestered until jury deliberations are completed. In addition to alleviating the possibility of tampering, the jury may also be sequestered to dilute the effects of pre-trial publicity.

Sequestration is the process whereby jurors are ordered to remain in virtual isolation during a trial. The court will order the jurors to remain in a hotel until the case is decided.

The jurors' contact with the outside world will be funneled through the court. The court will allow jurors to have only limited contact with their family members, and depending on the length of the trial, might provide conjugal visits with their spouses. The length of the sequestration varies depending on the nature of the case. Sequestration can last as little as a few days or, as with the Charles Manson and O.J. Simpson trials, the sequestration can last for more than nine months.

As is always the case in criminal trials, the judge must balance the need to protect jurors with the interests of the defendant to a fair trial. These are the factors the court will consider in making the determination about whether the jury needs protection and needs to sequestered:

1. The severity of the charge. The court is much more likely to sequester the jury in a capital murder case than in a larceny case. It is generally believed that the more the defendant has to lose, the more likely he might be to tamper with the jury. Sequestration may also be likely in cases involving organized crime and drug rings, and in other cases where there are large amounts of money at stake.

2. The effect sequestration will have on the proceedings. Judges like to preside over cases that proceed smoothly.

Sequestration can throw a few wrenches in the process because it requires the court and taxpayers to be responsible for the jurors twenty-four hours a day. That is why potential jurors can rest assured that before making the decision to sequester the court will carefully consider how sequestration will affect the case.

3. The level of publicity. The court will also sequester jurors to protect them from the influence of the media. The level of publicity is usually in direct proportion to the notoriety of the parties in the case.

4. Whether the defendant has a history of interfering or tampering with the jury. Courts realize that defendants who have previously tampered with or attempted to tamper with a jury are likely to do it again.

ANONYMOUS JURIES

Anonymous juries are impaneled in cases that require the court to go a step further in protecting jurors from tampering. The genesis of the anonymous jury can be traced back to the late 1950s. Anonymous juries are used to protect jurors from violence, the fear of violence, and the fear of retaliation. Anonymous juries can be impaneled at the request of the prosecutor's office, or the judge can use his own discretion.

Anonymous juries will allow individual jurors to serve in virtual anonymity. Their names, addresses, and phone numbers are concealed from the parties in the litigation as well as from the media. In anonymous juries, the jurors are given an exhaustive questionnaire designed to elicit the type of information needed to determine whether they possess any type of bias that would inhibit their ability to be impartial.

Sequestration and anonymous juries do not necessarily go hand in hand. Sequestration is often adequate in achieving the desired goals, but few anonymous juries serve without being sequestered. Some juries are ordered to serve in semi-sequestration. Although the jurors are not kept anonymous, it is possible that the judge can still order their first names and addresses be kept confidential.

The majority of criminal trials that use anonymous juries involve Racketeering Influenced and Corrupted Organizations (RICO) violations, or what are more commonly known as Mafia trials involving mobsters. Although courts first began using anonymous jurors in the federal prosecution of organized crime, they have also used them in some other popular cases, such as the federal case against police officers accused of beating Rodney King, and the trial of the individuals charged with the bombing of the World Trade Center in New York City.

Jurisdictions vary on when they will use an anonymous jury. The primary factors courts take into consideration when deciding whether to impanel an anonymous jury is whether there is a reasonable belief that jurors need protection. In instances where the court decides to impanel an anonymous jury, the court must take measures to ensure that this action does not prejudice the juror against the defendant. The following is an example of the standard explanation courts use to explain the use of anonymity: "[I]t is a common practice followed in many cases in the federal court to keep the names and the identities of the jurors in confidence. This is in no way unusual. It is a procedure being followed in this case to protect your privacy even from the Court."[8]

LESS RESTRICTIVE SECURITY MEASURES

Other security measures judges can take to protect jurors who have concerns about their safety include the following:

1. Increasing the presence of law enforcement personnel assigned to the trial.

2. Restraining the defendant.

3. Requiring people who enter the courtroom to be searched.

Jurors concerns about safety should not be suffered in silence. A juror who is concerned about his personal well-being cannot concentrate on the trial. If a juror feels influenced by an outside source, that fact should be brought to the judge's immediate attention. A concerned juror should persist until measures are taken to alleviate their concerns. Personal safety is something a juror should never allow to be the sole responsibility of someone else.

The Lighter Side of Jury Duty

Perhaps they feared for their safety or perhaps they just didn't want to serve on a jury and couldn't think of anything else to say. Whatever the reasons, here are the three worst excuses for avoiding jury duty:

1. My dog is pregnant.

2. My bad breath might offend the other members of the panel.

3. I am a lesbian who has been isolated, and therefore I no longer consider myself a U.S. citizen.

— *National Law Journal*, January 3, 1983

THE RIGHT TO NULLIFY 5

A jury's most significant right is also the one they are most likely to know nothing about: the power or right to nullify the law and follow their conscience when rendering their decisions. It is sometimes hard to convince novice jurors that this right exists, because judges often give instructions to the contrary.

The concept of jury nullification is not new to the legal scene. In the early nineteenth century in England, the majority of crimes carried an automatic death penalty sentence. Jurors who thought the penalty was too harsh simply failed to convict. When the juries ruled for an acquittal despite evidence to support a conviction, they were using nullification, although they had never been instructed of that right.

However, by all accounts, the idea of jury nullification began in 1649 at the trial of John Lilburne. Lilburne was charged with treason for publishing material that criticized the English government. Lilburne told the men who sat on his jury that they had the right to pass judgment on both the facts and the law of the case. The jury returned a not guilty verdict, as a guilty verdict would have meant a death sentence.

The first American trial to give rise to the concept of jury nullification involved the case of John Peter Zenger. Zenger was charged with seditious libel, or disseminating information designed to incite the overthrow of the government. Zenger printed a journal that published articles opposed to the governor of New York. Zenger had been hired by one of the governor's political foes. Zenger's attorney argued that the jury should have the right to determine the validity of the law as well as determine the facts. The jury found Zenger not guilty.

Today, jury nullification is a term that remains a mystery to the general public and the majority of people who serve on juries. However, its meaning is certainly alive and well in modern day jury deliberations, a fact that should come as no surprise when one considers the growing dissatisfaction many people feel toward the government and the legal system. This dissatisfaction is coupled with the feeling that legislatures are out of touch with the average man on the street, and that legislatures often enact laws prohibiting certain conduct members of the community don't agree should be unlawful. For example, in some communities such conduct might be physician-assisted suicide, in others it might be carrying a concealed weapon.

Newspapers are filled with stories about verdicts in high-profile cases that appear to reinforce the existence of jury nullification. Although every time the general public disagrees with a jury verdict does not necessarily mean the jury nullified the law. They may have just made a bad decision. One consequence of permitting cameras into the courtroom is that they allow the general public to stand over jurors' shoulders and second guess their every move.

The O.J. Simpson verdict invited a great deal of speculation. There were a few legal commentators who suggested that the decision in the trial was an example of jury nullification, a position that appears to be more deeply rooted in speculation than fact, and is evidence that many people do not clearly understand the meaning of jury nullification.

The twelve men and women who served on that jury clearly did not decide that murder was an acceptable act or that wealthy celebrity murderers should go unpunished. But there are many who would disagree with the O.J. Simpson jurors' claim that their decision was based on reasonable doubt. It is possible that their decision was intended to nullify police misconduct and to convey disapproval of police misbehavior.

One thing is certain, there is a swelling of support across the country for jury nullification. Evidence of it may have been seen in the following cases:

1. The jury appeared to forgive Oliver North for his part in the Iran-Contra affair. Perhaps, they disagreed with the law, but it is more likely that they did not approve of the conduct of North's superiors, who were insulated from prosecution.

2. The jury that presided over Washington, D.C., Mayor Marion S. Barry's case refused to convict him of felony drug charges despite the overwhelming evidence that supported

a conviction. It was reported that they did not like the way the federal government collected the evidence against Barry. The federal government's promises of sex to build its case was an affront to the jury's sense of justice and appropriate government conduct. So they ignored the evidence and the law and did what they thought was right.

3. The jury that heard the Bernard Goetz case decided not to follow the law and followed their conscience. Goetz was the New York City subway commuter charged with shooting a mugger in an act he said was self-defense.

4. The Rodney King jury might have used jury nullification, as well as the jury in the Reginald Denny case in which a bystander was beaten during the riots that followed the King verdict. The defendants despite being caught on tape, were acquitted of the serious charges and convicted of the lesser charges.

There are certainly countless other examples of jury nullification that never make the headlines. As jurors become more knowledgeable about their right to nullify the law and follow their conscience, jury nullification is sure to increase. Jurors cannot and should not be expected to operate like computers. They cannot be fed information and be expected to spit out decisions without feeling and thinking about them. It would be unconscionable for juries to do anything less than follow their conscience when what they decide can mean life or death, or jail or freedom.

It is important to note that the concept of jury nullification is actually only applicable in criminal cases in which the government is always a party and the question is always the same: Did the defendant violate the law? In most civil cases disputes will not involve the government as a party, and the question is often which party failed to act in accordance with the contracts, agreements or promises made between the two. Also, in civil cases there is no threat of jail or execution, so it is not as necessary for the jury to act as the conscience of the community. Another reason jury nullification is not applicable in civil trials is because the judge has the authority to modify or reject the jury's findings.

Jury nullification is not an example of renegade civilians attempting to overthrow the judicial system. It is a concept that is based on ideals that are as firmly entrenched in our society as the American flag or the Statute of Liberty. It is supported by sound legal authority. The United States Supreme Court has recognized that the jury is the conscience of the community, without fully embracing or memorializing the principal of jury nullification. In one U.S. Supreme Court case, in the dissenting opinion, it was held that jurors have the right to nullify the law but they don't have to be told of the right.[1]

However, the Supreme Court has stated that "juries are not bound by what seems inescapable logic to judges."[2] Moreover, Article XV, Section 5 of the Maryland Constitution states: "In the trial of all criminal cases, the Jury shall be the Judges of Law, as well as of fact, except that the Court may pass upon the sufficiency of the evidence to sustain a conviction." Indiana has a similar mandate in its constitution.

A federal appeals court held that, "If the jury feels the law is unjust, we recognize the undisputed power of the jury to acquit, even if its verdict is contrary to the law as given by a judge, and contrary to the evidence. If the jury feels that the law under which the defendant is accused is unjust, or that exigent circumstances justified the actions of the accused, or for any reason which appeals to their logic or passion, the jury has the power to acquit, and the courts must abide by that decision."[3]

Jury nullification is a necessary element of the legal system. Even the most staunch opposition to jury nullification must agree that in order for the legal system to remain a respected institution in our society, common citizens must believe that they have input and that there are appropriate checks on the government in enacting and enforcing laws. The legislature cannot write laws to cover all foreseeable situations and circumstances, thus jury nullification can serve as a safety net to protect someone from falling through the cracks. Jury nullification can protect defendants against a legislature that is out of touch with the man on the street or judges that are too rigid in their beliefs. Perhaps, as supporters of nullification have opined, if jury nullification were looked at as a means for jurors to temper justice with mercy, much of the opposition to jury nullification would be quieted.

The principle of jury nullification is not without limits. Jury nullification does not give jurors the right to behave irresponsibly. For example, many fear what would happen in a racist community, if juries decided they would convict every African-American charged with a crime, regardless of the evidence. The potential for these types of decisions is what frightens most people.

However, since judges retain the power to protect the innocent, they can take over if they find the jury's decision was irrational. Whenever the jury reaches a verdict that flies in the face of the evidence, the court can intervene by directing the verdict or granting a new trial. Thus, the concept of nullification does not allow the jury to pose a threat to innocent defendants. But jury nullification does protect citizens from legislatures that decided it is illegal to engage in conduct the majority of people consider acceptable, and it protects defendants from impassioned and heartless judges.

One reason there is mistrust of jury nullification is that jury nullification is not clearly understood. There is a fine distinction between what jurors can and cannot do. Juries cannot do any of the following:

1. They can't decide that a law is unconstitutional; they can say only that a defendant is not guilty of a particular crime. If a jury did declare a law unconstitutional, its decision would be inconsequential because its verdict only applies in the case over which it presides.

2. They can't make laws. Juries can't decide that a defendant is not guilty of the crime with which he is charged but find him guilty of a crime with which he is not charged. For example, if a defendant is charged with murder, the jury cannot find him not guilty of murder but guilty of rape.

3. They do not have the option of deciding what the law ought to be.

There are many people who fear jury nullification and insist it is a concept that a civilized society should denounce. Most fears are rooted in a general distrust for the common sense and integrity of the common man or woman; and the belief that nullification will lead to anarchy, because the average person is out of control and will act irresponsibly.

There are others who suggest that nullification will lead jurors to conceal their true feelings about subjects such as abortion and euthanasia during voir dire so they can be selected to serve on certain juries and advance their own agendas. There are also those who are fearful because jurors have little or no account-ability for acquittals in criminal cases.

Once the jury makes a decision to nullify a law and acquit a defendant, their decision is virtually final and cannot be attacked or overturned. Jurors are insulated from any legal ramifications of their decision. They cannot be sued or penalized because they deliberate in silence, and the closed jury room is not a place where the judge can tread to question them on their decision. It's not appropriate for the judge to ask questions about the nature of jury deliberations or how and why they reached a particular decision.

Moreover, the doctrine of double jeopardy precludes prosecutors from retrying or appealing a decision once the defendant has been acquitted. The prosecution cannot appeal a not guilty verdict in the same manner the defendant can appeal a guilty verdict.

The major critics of jury nullification continue to be prosecutors and judges who have a superiority complex, tend to be convinced of their own sanctity, and think they know what is best for everyone.

Because of fears associated with jury nullification, there is a big debate about whether jurors should be informed during standard jury instructions about their right to nullify. Jury instructions which are given at the close of evidence and before deliberations provide the framework within which jurors deliberate and fashion their verdict. They also provide juries with an outline of expected conduct. Only two states, Maryland and Indiana, have a constitutional mandate that requires nullification instructions. In other states, most courts are reluctant to thoroughly explain to jurors their option to apply the law to the facts. However, it is inappropriate for the judge to instruct jurors that they must decide a certain way if they find a certain set of facts.

Whether the jury is instructed on the issue of nullification is perhaps irrelevant, because people will not leave their conscience at the door. It is difficult to imagine that jurors who feel a strong pang of conscience would not find some way to justify reaching a verdict that was in line with it.

The Lighter Side of Jury Duty

One woman claimed her conscience would not allow her to serve on a jury because she possessed certain psychic powers that allowed her to foresee the outcome of the case. The judge bought it and excused her from service.

— *The National Law Journal,* August 4, 1986

The Right to Know What to Expect

6

The right to nullify is not the only jurors' right that is not fully acknowledged or embraced by the powers that be in the legal system. Another is the right to know what to expect from jury service. This is an important right and one that is recognized by those who are working hard to enact jury reform. There are many sound reasons why jurors should be informed and told what to expect before they begin jury service. These reasons include the following:

1. It alleviates the anxiety people experience when they first open their mailbox and realize they have been summoned for jury service. It is natural for human beings to feel uneasy about venturing into unknown areas.

2. It reduces the frustration jurors feel when they arrive for jury duty and find it's nothing like they expected. Juror frustration can carry over into their deliberations, and it might make jurors more likely to take measures to avoid future jury service.

3. Potential jurors might feel a greater sense of responsibility and commitment to a system they feel thinks enough of them to inform them of the road that lies ahead.

4. If potential jurors arrive knowing what to expect they can be better prepared to take the measures they need to alleviate any inconvenience or stress associated with jury service.

5. It is common courtesy. In a civilized society the government should not insist that its citizenry be required to do something without first and fully informing them of what is expected of them and what they can expect from their service.

WHAT TO EXPECT WHEN YOU ARE NOTIFIED

If you have never been summoned for jury service, you might not know how you will be notified. Generally, you can expect to receive a notice in your mailbox at least two weeks prior to the time when you are required to report. You can expect not to be called any more frequently than once every two years.

The summons will specifically state the time and date you are expected to report and the location where you are expected to report. If you have any doubts about when and where you are to report, the summons will usually include the name and telephone number of who you should contact with any questions or concerns. You should contact the number if you need directions or if you have a legitimate conflict that will make it impossible for you to appear on the date requested.

In some jurisdictions, the summons will include a telephone number to call the night before you are scheduled to report, to check to see if you still need to report the next day. Calling this number can save you a great deal of time and inconvenience.

If there is no number on the summons and you have a question or need to enter your excuse, contact the general information number for your local courthouse. After transferring you around the building a few times, you should be put in touch with someone who will be able to help you.

Expect a juror's summons to arrive when you least expect it and at the most inconvenient time possible.

What to Expect When You Arrive at the Courthouse

The first two things you should expect is that it will take longer to get to the courthouse than you anticipated, and the courthouse will have been relocated two blocks from where it was the last time you came down to pay a parking fine. When you finally arrive at the courthouse you will probably have difficulty locating a parking space. Most single-family dwellings have more parking spaces than those provided at courthouses. The spaces that are available will usually be located several blocks away and will cost you to use. To alleviate stress, follow these suggestions:

1. Allow extra time to locate parking, or better yet, drive to the courthouse over the weekend and check out the parking situation.

2. Bring along coins in case you have to feed a parking meter. Remember, you could possibly be in court all day. If you feed the meter for only two hours and return after eight hours, your car might be towed or you might receive a ticket. Don't expect to have time to feed the meter during the day. It may be best to find a parking lot where you take a ticket and pay whenever you leave, instead of using a parking meter and worry about whether you've put enough money in.

Once you find your way inside the courthouse, you might have difficulty finding your way around unless you are familiar with the building. Many courthouses do not have arrows to provide directions, and the room numbers are sometimes not posted in places where rational people would expect to find them. Fortunately, the main floor of most courthouses will have a locator board or an information desk that can point you in the direction of the jury assembly room. If not, approach someone who looks like they know their way around. People dressed in suits and carrying briefcases, and law enforcement personnel, are usually ripe sources of information. They spend lots of time at the courthouse and definitely know their way around.

When you finally locate the jury assembly room it will be filled with people sitting around trying to keep occupied. Usually within a half-hour of the time you were ordered to report a bailiff or other court personnel will appear and make some general announcement about how the selection process will begin. It is not reasonable to expect that just because you have been summoned that you will actually be called to hear a case.

A group of jurors will be called from the jury assembly room and escorted into the courtroom. They will be ushered into the jury box and the jury selection process will begin. After the voir dire, or jury selection process, if you are selected you will stay in the courtroom. If you are not selected, in most cases you will be excused and allowed to go home. However, in other instances you might have to undergo voir dire that will determine your qualification for another case.

There is no designated time from when you arrive at the courthouse to when you can be selected or excused from service. You can expect it to take several hours. It is not unusual for excused jurors to spend three or four hours at the courthouse. You should expect to spend a lot of time sitting around doing nothing. You should come to the courthouse armed with some things to keep you occupied, a good book or that needlepoint you have been meaning to finish. You will be discouraged from leaving the jury assembly room because you could be called at anytime, so it's also a good idea to bring along some snacks.

WHAT TO EXPECT DURING VOIR DIRE

The voir dire examination is the only opportunity jurors will be given to speak in open court. Here's a list of other things jurors can expect during voir dire:

1. It will last longer than you feel is necessary.

2. You will be asked questions that appear to have absolutely nothing to do with why you were summoned to appear. Although at this point you might not fully understand the nature of the case.

3. You will be asked questions that might appear to be an unnecessary invasion of your privacy and that you might be reluctant to answer.

4. Depending on the nature of the case, the courtroom might or might not be filled with spectators.

5. The lawyers might appear to argue about whether you or other jurors should be allowed to serve.

6. You might be asked to fill out a questionnaire, in addition to being asked to answers questions in open court. The questionnaires vary in length. However, they usually include about 100 questions, although the jurors in the O.J. Simpson case were required to answer more than 300 questions.

7. The lawyers at times might appear to be condescending and talking down to you, and at other times they might appear arrogant and self-absorbed.

8. You might hear very creative responses from fellow potential jurors who are trying hard to ensure that they will be excused from service.

> ### Why does a *petit jury* usually have twelve jurors?
>
> No one knows for sure. Some historians suggest that the twelve-person jury is rooted in religion. Solomon had twelve officers, Jacob had twelve sons, and there were twelve apostles. Others suggest a more practical reason. They contend that twelve is a sufficient number to reflect a consensus of the community sentiment, but it is not sufficient to create a riot if the panel is unable to reach an agreement.
>
> — *Valparaiso Law Review*, Fall 1966

WHAT TO EXPECT DURING TRIAL

There are a few things you can expect once the trial begins.

1. You can expect the judge to ask you to get up and leave the jury box and return to the jury deliberation room each time you start to get comfortable. This could happen several times depending on the length of the trial. Whenever the lawyers need to discuss something that the judge has not allowed into evidence, the jurors must leave the room to allow the lawyers and judge to discuss these matters.

2. Throughout the trial you can expect to be constantly reminded not to discuss the case with anyone and not to make up your mind until the case closes.

3. The lawyers and the judge might have private discussions at the bench outside of the jury's hearing. Again, they are discussing matters that have not been admitted into evidence and they fear might improperly influence your decision.

4. The lawyers may appear to repeat themselves. It is not just an appearance; they often do repeat themselves in an effort to drive home certain points.

5. You might have a difficult time remaining focused on the evidence. Trials can drag on for long periods. However, if the judge notices jurors eyes beginning to glass over, she will usually call a recess and allow jurors to get up and stretch their legs.

6. You may have difficulty understanding the evidence. Jurors are often asked to sit on cases in which there is a presentation of highly technical evidence.

7. You can expect the case to take a lot longer than the lawyers and judge project at the beginning of the case.

8. The lawyers' opening statements don't really help you in understanding the nature of the case.

9. The case might close and you still might have many unanswered questions.

10. Expect the trial not to begin on time and to be periodically interrupted because the judge or lawyers have to take care of other commitments.

11. Expect that no one will seem to be working to make your life easier.

The *Perry Mason* Instruction

Jurors are sometimes instructed not to expect someone to jump up and confess to the crime; that only happens on Perry Mason. This instruction began being given to jurors because defense lawyers feared many convictions came about because no one else came forth and admitted to the crime in the way that happens on television.

WHAT TO EXPECT AFTER THE CASE IS CLOSED

When both sides rest and the case is closed you can expect to be happier than you thought you would be, but this is where the hard work really begins. Here is what you can expect:

1. The closing arguments take longer and create more confusion than they actually clear up for you.

2. You might have no idea how you plan to decide, or you might have firmly entrenched beliefs about the defendant's guilt or innocence.

3. The instructions the judge gives on how you should consider the evidence would probably be confusing. The judge will ask if you have any questions, and his answers might do little to clear up the confusion. There are very rigid guidelines as to what judges can and cannot say.

4. Other members of the jury panel might have very different opinions from yours. You might even wonder if they sat through the same trial you did. That discrepancy can be expected when you have a group of people with different backgrounds and experiences thrown together. However,

each person's ideas should be thoughtfully considered in reaching the decision. Does that mean you should expect every member of the jury panel to be thoughtful and considerate? You should expect it, but don't be too surprised if that is not the case. Albert Camus said, "it takes all kinds to make a world," and I'm suggesting that it also takes all kinds to make a jury that reflects a cross section of a community. Remembering why you have been drawn together will go a long way in helping you cope with difficult members of the panel.

5. The deliberation process or the time it takes to reach a decision is difficult to gauge, so you should keep an open mind and try not to squeeze it into a certain time frame. The fact that the case took several months does not mean the deliberation will take a similar length of time, and the fact that the trial wrapped up in a few hours does not necessarily mean you will be home in time for dinner. The length of deliberation depends in large part on what you are being asked to decide. It might also depend on whether you are required to reach a unanimous verdict—in which everyone must vote the same way—or whether only a majority decision is required. Often, hung juries—when the jury is unable to reach a verdict—take the longest time because it takes a while for a jury to conclude that it will be unable to reach a verdict. When that information is reported to the judge, he will send the jury back into the deliberation room and ask that it continue deliberating until it is able to reach a verdict. The judge might do this a few times before he accepts the fact that the jury is unable to reach a decision.

6. During the course of deliberation you might change your mind once or several times on certain matters, based on what you hear from other members of the panel.

7. You will receive very strong reactions from both sides of the case when your decision is read aloud. Emotional outbursts from the victim's families or the parties involved in the litigation are not unusual. They may seek out opportunities to discuss your decision, to ask questions or to thank you for deciding the way you did. Jurors have different attitudes about these overtures. There have been cases in which jurors sought out the victims and the parties to offer condolences. There was also a reported case in which the jurors took up a collection of money for one of the victims. Depending on the nature of the case, you will probably experience a very emotional reaction when this important work is concluded and you leave people you have spent lots of time with.

8. The judge will thank you for the time and effort you put into the case and, quite unceremoniously, bid you a fair adieu. No matter how important your task, there will be no fanfare or parades in your honor. You can expect the end of the case to be somewhat anticlimactic.

9. In a high-profile case, the media will probably contact you for interviews. However, in most routine cases this is not to be expected.

10. Your opinion of the judicial system will probably change, and according to most studies it will change for the better.

The judge, lawyers, and bailiff are the people you will encounter during the course of the trial. Their roles are quite different, but they each will have a great impact on your jury service.

WHAT TO EXPECT FROM THE JUDGE

The judge will work very hard to maintain his distance from members of the jury, which should not necessarily be construed as rudeness or arrogance, although it might appear that way. Judges attempt to retain their distance to ensure that they maintain their professional integrity, and to show their impartiality and avoid even the appearance of impropriety. The defendant might interpret the judge's friendliness as an attempt to influence the jury.

It is a well-established principle in law that contact between the judge and the jury should be limited in the following ways:

1. It is within the court's discretion whether or not to respond to a juror's question or request.

2. The judge should confer with the lawyers before responding to a juror.

3. The contact between judge and jury should only take place in open court. There should be no private communications in chambers or elsewhere.

4. In federal cases, the judge might ask the jury if they are deadlocked and encourage them to try to reach a verdict. However, the judge should not try to determine the

substance of juror deliberations or which way their vote is going.

WHAT TO EXPECT FROM THE LAWYERS

As is the case with judges, lawyers are also bound to maintain their professional distance for juries. Lawyers will not speak to jurors directly, and their only communication with jurors should take place in open court. Jurors are generally issued badges that identify them as jurors, in the event they run into an attorney in the bathroom or cafeteria during a recess in the trial.

Again, a lawyer's indifference should not be misconstrued, as they are also bound to avoid the appearance of impropriety. Jurors should not expect lawyers to initiate any contact or communication with you during the trial. After the trial ends, lawyers might approach the judge about discussing the decision with the jury.

Also, lawyers have different styles of trying a case. Some are subdued, while others can be flashy in their manner and appearance. So jurors can't really know what to expect from the lawyers until the case begins. However, jurors should strive to look beyond the lawyers and focus on the evidence being presented. Remember, the lawyer is not on trial; the issues are. Don't let a lawyer who rubs you the wrong way interfere with your decision making.

WHAT TO EXPECT FROM THE BAILIFF

The bailiff, who is usually a member of the local sheriff's department, is the person in the courtroom with whom you will have the most direct contact and communication. Bailiffs often serve as the link between you and the judge. If you have any questions or concerns, they should be directed to the bailiff, who will inform the judge. Also, when you reach the verdict you will first inform the bailiff, who will notify the judge.

Your conversations and contact with the bailiff should be restricted to matters that are not directly related to the case. It is inappropriate to discuss the case with the bailiff.

If you expect the unexpected, your jury experience will be a lot more manageable.

The Lighter Side of Jury Duty

In a Texas case, too few people responded to the jury summons to impanel a jury. To clear his docket, the judge exercised his authority under an old Texas statute to round up people off the street and force them to serve as jurors. The bailiff was ordered to go out in search of jurors and not to return without a jury. The bailiff returned with eighteen men from the local mission that provided lodging to homeless men. As the men all had the same address and no occupation, the voir dire was soon completed and the case proceeded to a swift conclusion.

— *Litigation*, Fall 1984

JUROR RESPONSIBILITIES 7

A recitation of rights without any mention of obligation or responsibility is sorely lacking. Rights sustain their viability because they are rooted in responsibility. Parents have the right to raise their children but they are also obligated for their children's support and have the responsibility of ensuring that they receive emotional, spiritual, and physical guidance. The same principles apply to jurors. For each of the rights outlined in this book, there are implied responsibilities.

The integrity of the judicial system relies on jurors who exercise their rights and responsibilities with honor and integrity. This should be viewed as more than a cliché, when you consider the importance of the task jurors have been summoned to undertake. A husband might ask the jury to decide what should happen to his wife who has been accused of killing their two children. A mother might ask the jury to compensate her for the loss of a child, whose death was due to the negligence of a manufacturer of a child safety seat. Jurors must never lose sight of how monumentally important their job is to other people who rely on them, and they should consider what they would expect of people that were summoned to decide their fate or the fate of someone they love.

RESPONSIBILITIES AND THE RIGHT TO SERVE

Jurors have a responsibility to respond to the jury summons and to appear in court on the designated date at the designated time. Many people ignore the summons, assuming that the system is too busy dealing with rapists and murderers to do anything about their failure to appear. People also assume that if they do not show up, someone else will and no one will be harmed by their absence. However, it is not fair for a person to pass on their responsibility to someone else or suggest that their presence will not make a difference. If the system is to work, we all must accept responsibility for doing our part. A person's presence could make the difference between a hung jury and a jury that is able to reach a fair and sound verdict that is in the interest of justice. Juries are supposed to reflect a cross section of the community. If large groups of people avoid service, it will be impossible to achieve the cross-section and apply the safety valve it places on the system.

As a juror, you also have a responsibility to respond honestly to the questions they are asked on voir dire. This is so because false answers could lead to your being held in contempt, and responding honestly is the right thing to do. You should tell the truth even if, as a consequence, you are not selected to serve on a jury. Being responsible in responding to the summons does not mean you should expect to be allowed to serve. Your only obligation is to show up and tell the truth. It is as equally important to tell the truth about your criminal record and income, or things that can be easily verified, as it is to tell the truth about your health or other things that might impair your ability to serve, such as difficulty with reading, writing, or understanding English. You can not carry out your responsibilities as a juror if you cannot understand what's going on around you.

Jurors are supposed to come to jury service with a blank slate. You should be honest about any preconceived notions you have about the outcome of the case, or about who is or is not telling the truth. You should also be honest in disclosing your attitudes about the case, feelings of empathy toward parties in the case, or previous jury experience on similar type of cases that might have tainted your ability to serve. Usually, the only way this type of information is uncovered is if you disclose the information and you have a responsibility to do so.

You cannot possibly remain impartial in a case when you have something vested in the outcome of the case. Placing wagers on the case or serving on a jury when you have a personal or business relationship with the parties is irresponsible. Moreover, it would be reprehensible for a juror to serve on a case in which he allowed his deep-seated feelings, racial or sexual biases, or personal feelings about certain crimes such as rape or sexual harassment, or defenses such as insanity or battered woman syndrome, to cloud his judgment and interfere with his ability to give the defendant a fair trial.

One of the greatest criticisms of the O.J. Simpson jury was that it took only four hours to consider a case that took almost a year to present. A juror's biggest responsibility is to remain attentive during the trial, not allow her mind to wander, and to remain focused on the evidence and facts presented. Jurors can then proceed to the jury deliberation room with an open mind and engage in thoughtful consideration of everything that was presented during the trial.

Jurors have a responsibility to reach their own decision based on their analysis of the evidence and the points brought out during the deliberation. Jurors should not give in to undue influence from other jurors and allow themselves to be forcefully swayed from their decision. Jurors should have the strength of character to stand by a decision, even one that might result in a hung jury. And although judges will encourage juries to reach a verdict, jurors must allow their own conscience to guide them in making decisions.

If any misconduct takes place in jury room—for example, if there is evidence of jurors using drugs or alcohol in the jury room or if there is no deliberation and the jurors reach a decision by flipping a coin—it is incumbent on any juror with integrity to bring this information to the judge's attention. Telling the judge might not be a popular stance, but it is an appropriate and responsible one.

RESPONSIBILITIES AND THE RIGHT TO PRIVACY

A juror's right to privacy is an important one. However, there is a potential for jurors to use that right for reasons other than which it was intended. For instance, jurors have a responsibility not to hide behind their right to privacy to avoid answering certain questions, to avoid jury service, or to increase their chances of serving on a jury. It is irresponsible to use this right for the wrong reasons. Again, this point must be made: It does not matter if you never get to sit on a jury, what matters is that you show up and tell the truth. Lying is lying whether by omission or admission. Refusing to answer questions because you claim they are an affront to your right to privacy is a lie when, in fact, you do not wish to answer the questions for other reasons.

This doesn't mean if you feel a question is an affront to your privacy that you should not exercise your right to privacy. However, before you do so, you should carefully consider your motives and consider whether doing so would be acting responsibly. Also, ask yourself if you really care whether anyone knows your television habits or if you are refusing to answer the question just to make a point, and if so, is making the point really important enough to slow down the wheels of justice and prolong the parties' chance of having their case heard and grievances addressed. The analysis would be same even if you are asked about your sexual habits, but understandably your conclusion might be completely different.

If you decide your privacy is being invaded, you have the responsibility not to lie but to bring this concern to the judge's attention and cooperate with the court in trying to satisfy your concerns and ensure your privacy. However, making false privacy claims can have the same result as pulling fire alarms when there is no fire. Judges might begin to ignore the calls or be slow to respond to legitimate privacy concerns.

RESPONSIBILITIES AND THE RIGHT TO SAFETY

Closely related to the responsibilities associated with the right to privacy are the responsibilities associated with the right to safety. The right to be safe while serving on a jury is an important consideration. However, it would be irresponsible for a juror to claim irrational fears for their safety to avoid jury service. If a juror has legitimate concerns about safety, he is responsible for bringing those concerns to the presiding judge's immediate attention.

Jurors also are responsible for informing the judge if they have any suspicions of jury tampering. If jurors have been offered bribes, been threatened to decide a certain way, or received threatening phone calls, the judge should be made aware of these incidents.

Jurors should also inform the judge if they receive any third-party contact or communication that they believe is intended to influence their decision, even if it's seemingly harmless. A note, a look, or a gesture might make jurors feel uncomfortable. They should not take anything for granted and should follow their instincts. If they feel uncomfortable, it will be difficult to focus on the evidence and engage in open and honest deliberations.

Bringing information of suspected tampering to the judge's attention does not necessarily mean a juror will be dismissed or any action will be taken. However, if there is a threat to the jurors' safety, the sooner the judge becomes aware of it the sooner the judge can take appropriate action to ensure that no injury or harm comes to anyone.

RESPONSIBILITIES AND THE RIGHT TO NULLIFY

The responsibilities associated with the right to nullify could arguably be described as the most important responsibilities jurors carry with them into the deliberation room. The right to nullify carries with it the right to follow one's conscience. However, jurors have to be certain their consciences are clear.

It is irresponsible for people to seek out jury service as an opportunity to advance their own agendas. If a juror's conscience is not clear, her decision will certainly be tainted, and the members of the community will have to suffer the consequences of her behavior.

Jury nullification has potential for abuse, like many other things in our society. However, it is each individual juror's responsibility to ensure that there are no abuses. Jurors can do so by giving thoughtful consideration to their decision and not succumbing to irrational pressure that might be exerted by other members of the jury.

Jury nullification ensures that members of our society retain the power to act mercifully toward their neighbors, if their consciences and hearts dictate them to do so. However, if jury nullification is used or misused unconsciously, without thought it can lose its place of distinction. If we allow that to happen, we all would lose.

Responsibilities and the Right to Compensation

Money not only corrupts, it corrupts thoroughly. The lack of money and the possibility of money can corrupt the purest of souls. However, people of character must serve as bulwarks against corruption.

The greatest responsibility associated with the right to compensation is to avoid allowing the paltry fees or the possibility of a larger pay day to influence one's performance as a juror. For instance, rushing through the deliberations, or agreeing with a decision that you know is not appropriate because you want to get back to your job and receive a living wage, would not be responsible and would pose a great threat to the integrity of the legal system. Equally irresponsible would be allowing the possibility of an appearance on *The Oprah Winfrey Show* or capturing the headlines of the *National Enquirer* to disrupt your concentration and affect the way you perform as a juror.

Jury service is a privilege of citizenship in this country and one that few other countries allow their citizenry to enjoy. It is also one of the privileges that, if lost, would be sorely missed and cause this country to be held in less esteem in the eyes of people around the world who long to live here.

Jurors who assume the responsibility of serving on a jury have the immense responsibility of giving jury duty their very best effort. It should be approached with a sincerity and professionalism that one would approach any other important task she undertakes, whether it is running a business, raising children, or performing a job. We do not operate in a vacuum.

Everything we do touches someone else and affects their life, and this is definitely true of jury duty. Each individual juror must decide what affect his service will have on others.

The Lighter Side of Jury Duty

After twenty hours of deliberations, tempers in the jury room began to flare and one juror became so overwhelmed by the debate that she locked herself in the bathroom and refused to participate any further. The judge was forced to declare a mistrial.

— *National Law Journal*, January 14, 1985

JURY REFORMS 8

Everyone who has responded to a jury summons or knows of someone who has responded to a jury summons has a story to tell that might be titled "Hurry up and Wait!" Every story includes a tale of a juror rushing down to the courthouse, spending a half-hour trying to find a parking space, waiting for the elevator and rushing to the jury assembly room where jurors sit all day before being sent home without ever hearing a case. This is not everyone's experience with jury duty, but similar stories fill the air. Fortunately, the horizon is filled with proposed reforms intended to improve jury duty and to make jurors experiences more meaningful, pleasurable, and effective. Local bar associations in more than half the states are considering ways to improve jury service. These reforms include but are certainly not limited to the following:

1. Briefing jurors on what they can expect from jury service. This may seem like a small point, but it is a very important one. The majority of frustrations first-time jurors experience is brought on by their expectations not meeting

reality. Most of what people who have not served on juries know about jury duty is what they have seen on television. Whether the source is real-life Court TV or L.A. Law reruns, the image portrayed is inaccurate. If jurors were told that they should expect to wait around for long periods or that they might spend the entire day at the courthouse without ever being called, they could prepare themselves accordingly and not get so frustrated by their jury duty experience.

2. Minimizing legalese. Jurors are lay members of the legal system. They have no reason to know the difference between the legal concepts of *assumption of the risk* and *contributory negligence*. However, they are constantly bombarded with language and terms they do not understand and are expected to make sound and rational decisions based on the information presented. There is a loud cry for requiring lawyers to use plain English when addressing jurors and presenting cases.

3. Providing a written copy of instructions. At the conclusion of the presentation of evidence, the judge will turn to the jury to give them instructions to use as a guide in reaching their decision. Large portions of the jury instructions will be taken directly from the statutes, a sure guarantee that the instructions will be drenched in legal doublespeak. Today, in the majority of cases, jurors are given oral instructions and then asked if they have questions. Jurors probably don't have questions while they are in the jury box, although they might just be too embarrassed to show confusion in open court. However, they will certainly have

questions during the deliberations when they are trying to recall all of the evidence presented, as well as the instructions given by the judge. Providing jurors with written instructions, instead of just oral instructions, will give them an opportunity to more thoughtfully consider their decision. With the written instructions in front of them, jurors will be able to read them at their leisure and ensure that they have a full understanding of what they are being asked to do.

Some jurisdictions, such as Illinois, require jury instructions in criminal cases be in writing. In some other jurisdictions, such as Indiana, there is a prohibition against written jury instructions. In federal cases, the trial court has the discretion whether or not to use written jury instructions.

4. Allowing jurors to ask questions. Jurors are the only trial participants who are not allowed to ask the witness questions. That sounds ludicrous when you consider that the jury will have the responsibility of making a decision. If jurors don't have a full understanding of what the witness is saying, how can they be expected to make a sound decision? Jurors can't rely on the attorneys to ask all the appropriate questions because attorneys ask only questions to which they know the answers and that will assist in supporting their case. Allowing jurors to ask questions does not mean they will be permitted to examine witnesses. What is being proposed would allow jurors to write their questions and give them to the bailiff, who will pass them to judge. The judge will review the questions, and if they

don't violate any of the rules of evidence, he will ask the questions and order the witness to respond.

5. Limiting term of service. One reason jurors avoid jury service is because they fear being selected for a trial that lasts for several weeks or possibly months. Eight states have adopted a one-day, one-trial policy. When jurors are summoned, they will be notified that they will only be required to serve for one day. If they are not selected to serve during that day, they will be released from duty.

6. Limiting the number of peremptory challenges. This change will expedite the voir dire process. Many people are surprised that it often takes longer to select the jury than it does to try the case. Attorneys try to select a jury that is favorable to their cause as opposed to one that is impartial. Sitting around waiting for a jury to be impaneled accounts for much of the time associated with jury service. The court will summon more jurors than it needs. Ordinarily, excess jurors will not be released until a jury has been impaneled in each of the cases that are ready for trial.

7. Many states are considering going to the federal method of voir dire, in which the attorneys submit questions to the judge and the judge examines the potential jurors. This is considered another means of expediting the trial process and more efficiently managing the use of jurors' time.

8. Allowing jurors to discuss the trial proceedings among themselves during the trial. Jurors are admonished not to discuss the case among themselves until they enter the jury deliberation room. This is true even in cases in which they

have been sequestered and thrown together for nine months. This reform is considered controversial. However, jurors would be given instructions throughout the trial to help guide their discussions and would be again admonished not to make up their minds about the case until the close of the evidence. This reform is intended to make the deliberation more meaningful. Besides, since jurors are bombarded with information, it makes sense that they would want to share their thoughts with the other members of the jury.

9. Allowing jurors to take notes. Generally, judges and lawyers can take notes during trial, but jurors cannot. Some jurisdictions allow note taking, or give the judge the discretion to decide whether to allow note taking. The ban against note taking originated at a time when the jury pool was mostly illiterate, and there was a. concern that jurors who could write would have an undue influence on those who could not. Three present-day concerns are that notes might be inaccurate, note taking might be distracting to the other jurors or the attorneys and, jurors taking notes might not be paying attention to what is being presented.

10. Creating an "ombudservice" for prospective jurors. The first such service was created in Manhattan, New York. The service, which operates independently of the court system, has a booth set up in the hallway near the main jury assembly room in the courthouse. It also operates a twenty-four-hour jury hotline number. The service assists jurors with all kinds of problems, ranging from assisting people with

understanding exemptions to assisting potential jurors who do not understand English.

11. The Fully Informed Jury Association is hard at work throughout the country seeking state statutes or Constitutional amendments that would require judges and allow attorneys to instruct jurors of their rights and responsibilities, especially the right to nullify.

Juror reform is gaining momentum throughout the country. Organizations such as Ralph Nader's Center for the Study of Responsive Law, the National Association of Civil Jurors, the American Bar Association, and the Brookings Institution have their hands in the push for reform. In the not-so-distant future, we can realistically expect significant changes in jury service, and most of those changes will be for the better.

The Lighter Side of Jury Duty

In a Lansing, Michigan case, a juror noticed one of the witnesses wearing a pair of boots that had recently been stolen from the juror's home. During a recess, the juror approached the judge and told him about his stolen boots. The judge ordered the witness to remove the boots and charged him with theft. The judge was then forced to declare a mistrial.

— *National Law Journal*, March 31, 1986

GLOSSARY

acquittal. The determination that the defendant in a criminal case is not guilty and should be released from custody.

alternate juror. A juror that substitutes for a juror who is unable to serve or is excused from service.

bailiff. A member of the sheriff's department assigned to serve in the courtroom.

challenge for cause. An objection to allowing a prospective juror to serve because there is a specific reason they are not qualified to serve.

contempt of court. Conduct which has a tendency to impede the administration of justice or the failure to comply with a judge's order.

coroner's jury. A jury convened to determine the cause of death being investigated in a criminal homicide case.

court reporter. A stenographer who records the proceedings in a court of law.

deliberation. See *jury deliberation.*

district attorney. The title given in some states to the state or county attorney responsible for prosecuting all those accused of crimes.

grand jury. The jury that is responsible for examining the charges against a person accused of a crime and for deciding whether there is sufficient evidence to bring formal charges.

hung jury. A jury that is unable to reach a verdict.

impanel. The method by which juror's are selected and sworn to serve.

in chambers. This refers to the judge's office, as opposed to the judge's courtroom. Confidential conferences with the attorneys in a case are frequently held in chambers. (also called *in camera*).

jury box. The section of the courtroom where jurors sit during the court proceedings.

jury deliberations. The juror's formal discussion and debate of the issue in the case.

jury foreperson. The spokesperson for the jury. The foreperson is selected by a vote of the jurors.

jury instructions. The directions the judge gives the jury to guide their debate and discussion of the law, facts and other evidence.

jury panel. Group of persons who have been summoned for jury duty and the group from which the jury will be selected.

jury sequestration. The isolation of juror's from the general public and the parties in the case.

jury tampering. Any unauthorized contact or communication with the jury which is designed to influence their decision.

mistrial. A trial that is terminated without a verdict due to an error or misconduct in the proceedings, or due to a hung jury.

open court. This refers to the official court proceedings that are held in front of the jury, as opposed to matters discussed in chambers or at a side bar.

panel. See *jury panel*.

peremptory challenge. An objection to allowing a prospective juror to serve that does not require an explanation or a specific basis for making the challenge.

petit jury. A jury, usually of twelve persons, that decides the facts in a criminal or civil case at trial. It is called a *petit* jury to distinguish it from a *grand* jury.

polling the jury. A practice which takes place after the jury foreman announces the verdict where the judge asks each individual juror how they voted. This is usually done at the request of one of the attorneys in order to assure that the jurors all agree on the verdict.

prosecutor or **prosecuting attorney.** The title used in some states for the state or county attorney who prosecutes persons accused of crimes. In other state the term *district attorney* may be used, and the title in the federal system is *U.S. Attorney.*

sidebar. A conference which takes place between the judge and attorney's in the courtroom but away from the hearing of the jury or witnesses.

summons. A written directive from a court, ordering prospective juror's to appear under penalty of fine or imprisonment for failure to do so.

U.S. Attorney. An attorney employed by the federal government who is responsible for prosecuting persons accused of federal crimes.

venire. The process by which jurors are summoned for jury duty.

verdict. A judge's or jury's finding or decision.

voir dire. The examination or interview of prospective juror's to determine whether they are qualified to serve on a jury.

APPENDIX A
LANDMARK JURY-RELATED
COURT DECISIONS

The following are some significant United States Supreme Court decisions relating to juries. The title of the case is given, followed by the citation and a brief summary of what the court decided. The citation tells where the full text of the court's written decision may be found. "U.S." stands for the set of books called *United States Reports*, which contain the opinions of the United States. Supreme Court. The numbers give the volume number, the page number, and the year the case was decided. For example, the first case listed below is titled *Strauder v. West Virginia*. The citation tells you that the court's opinion can be found in Volume 100 of the *United States Reports* at page 303, and it was decided in the year 1880.

Strauder v. West Virginia, 100 U.S. 303 (1880)—The exclusion of black men from grand and petit juries on the basis of their race was a denial of equal protection under the law as guaranteed by the 14th Amendment.

Callan v. Wilson, 127 U.S. 540 (1888)—Petty offenses do not require a jury.

Smith v. Texas, 311 U.S. 128 (1940)—Juries must reflect a fair cross section of the community.

Ballard v. United States, 329 U.S. 187 (1946)—The exclusion of women violated the concept of a representative jury.

Swain v. Alabama, 380 U.S. 202 (1965)—This case is the controlling authority for a constitutional claim against the discriminatory use of peremptory challenges.

Duncan v. Louisiana, 391 U.S. 145 (1968)—A jury trial is required in all criminal cases in which the penalty could exceed six months.

William v. Florida, 399 U.S. 78 (1970)—A twelve person jury is not constitutionally mandated.

Johnson v. Louisiana, 406 U.S. 356 (1972)—Less than unanimous verdicts are permissible.

Ballew v. Georgia, 435 U.S. 223 (1978)—A six member jury satisfies the Sixth Amendment but anything less than six does not.

Kentucky v. Whorton, 441 U.S. 786 (1979)—A jury charge addressing the presumption of innocence need not always be given to the jury as part of the standard jury instructions.

Baston v. Kentucky, 476 U.S. 79 (1986)—Criminals have a right to juries in which members of their group are not excluded, and all individuals have a right to be included in the jury pool.

Appendix B
Juror Compensation and Punishment for Failing to Respond to Summons

This appendix contains a list of the amount of juror compensation paid in federal and state courts, and the punishment for a juror who fails to appear when called for jury duty. The symbol "§" stands for *section*. Unless otherwise noted, the full title of the set of laws is given in the section on compensation, and is abbreviated in the section on punishment. While every effort has been made to provide current information as of the date of publication of this book, you must be aware that the law is subject to change at any time.

Federal District Courts

Compensation: $40 per day for the first 30 days, then an additional $10 per day at the discretion of the court; + travel, compensation for toll roads, etc. Title 28, United States Code, §1871.

Punishment: $100 max. fine and/or 3 days max. incarceration. 28 U.S.C. §1866(g).

ALABAMA

Compensation: $10 per day + $.05 per mile. If juror is employed, employer is required to pay regular pay minus $10 paid by state for first 3 days. Code of Alabama, §12-19-210.

Punishment: Contempt of court and/or $100 max. fine and/or 10 days incarceration. C.A. §12-16-82.

ALASKA

Compensation: $25 per day + travel and per diem of state employees. Alaska Rules of Administration, Rule 14.

Punishment: Contempt of court; $300 max. fine and/or 6 months max. incarceration. Alaska Statutes, §§09.50.010 & 09.50.020.

ARIZONA

Compensation: $12 per day + mileage of state employees. Arizona Revised Statutes Annotated, §21-221.

Punishment: Contempt of court; $100 max. fine. A.R.S. §21-334.

ARKANSAS

Compensation: $20 per day. Arkansas Code of 1987 Annotated, §16-34-103.

Punishment: Not less than $5 or more than $500 fine. A.C.A. §16-32-106(d).

CALIFORNIA

Compensation: $5 per day + $.15 per mile. California Code of Civil Procedure, §215.

Punishment: Contempt of court punishable by fine and/or incarceration. Cal. Code Civ. Proc., §209.

COLORADO

Compensation: Employer pays minimum of $50 per day for the first 3 days if the person is *regularly employed*, then the state pays $50 per day. Statutes defines *regular employment* as including "part-time, temporary, and casual employment if the employment hours may be determined by a schedule, custom, or practice established during the three-month period preceding the juror's term of service." Colorado Revised Statutes Annotated, §§13-71-126 to 13-71-129.

Punishment: Class 3 misdemeanor. C.R.S.A. §18-8-612.

CONNECTICUT

Compensation: Employer pays regular salary for the first 5 days for person who are employed "full-time," then the state pays $50 per day. If unemployed or not full-time employed, state reimburses juror for out-of-pocket expenses (not including food) including 20¢ per mile for travel, but in no event less than $20 nor more than $50 per day. Law contains complex definitions and qualifications, and when employer may be exempted. Connecticut General Statutes Annotated, §51-247.

Punishment: $90 fine. C.G.S.A. §51-237.

DELAWARE

Compensation: $20 per day + travel. Delaware Code Annotated, Title 10, §4514.

Punishment: Criminal contempt with $100 max. fine and/or 3 days max. incarceration. D.C.A. Title 10, §4516.

FLORIDA

Compensation: $15 for the first 3 days, then $30 per day thereafter; except no state compensation is paid for the first 3 days if the juror receives his or her regular pay from an employer. Florida Statutes, §40.24.

Punishment: $100 max. fine. Fla. Stat., §40.23.

GEORGIA

Compensation: Not less than $5 per day or more than $35 per day. Official Code of Georgia Annotated, §15-12-7.

Punishment: Contempt of court. C.G.A. §15-12-10.

HAWAII

Compensation: $30 per day + $.33 per mile. Hawaii Revised Statutes, §612-8(a).

Punishment: Contempt of court. H.R.S. §612-19.

IDAHO

Compensation: $10 per day + mileage of county employees. Idaho Code §2-215.

Punishment: Criminal contempt with $100 max. fine and/or 3 days max. incarceration. Idaho Code §2-217.

ILLINOIS

Compensation: $4, $5, or $10 per day, depending on the county + mileage (but not more than $15). Illinois Annotated Statutes, Chapter 55, §5/4-1101.

Punishment: Contempt of court; $5 min. fine and $100 max. fine. I.A.S., Ch. 55, §305/15.

INDIANA

Compensation: $15 per day until impaneled, then $40 per day, + mileage at rate paid to state officers. Indiana Code Annotated, §33-19-1-4.

Punishment: Criminal contempt. I.C.A. §33-4-5.5-10.

IOWA

Compensation: $10 per day + mileage + reimbursement for actual expenses. Iowa Code Annotated, §607A.8.

Punishment: Contempt of court. I.C.A. §607A.36.

KANSAS

Compensation: $10 per day + mileage. Kansas Statutes Annotated, §43.171.

Punishment: $100 max. fine. K.S.A. §43.165.

KENTUCKY

Compensation: $12.50 to $25 per day, depending on the court. Kentucky Revised Statutes Annotated, §29A.330.

Punishment: Contempt of court. K.R.S. §29A.150.

LOUISIANA

Compensation: Not less than $12 or more than $25 per day + mileage. Louisiana Revised Statutes Annotated, §3049B.

Punishment: $50 max. fine and/or 3 days max. incarceration. L.S.A. §3049A.

MAINE

Compensation: $10 per day + $.15 per mile. Maine Revised Statutes Annotated, Title 14, §1215.

Punishment: $100 max. fine and/or 3 days max. incarceration. M.R.S.A., Title 14, §1217.

MARYLAND

Compensation: $10 to 15 per day (depending upon the county) + mileage. Annotated Code of Maryland, Courts and Judicial Procedure, §8-106.

Punishment: $100 max. fine and/or 3 days max. incarceration. A.C.M., Cts. & Jud. Proc. §8-401.

MASSACHUSETTS

Compensation: $16 per day in first degree murder cases, $14 per day in all others, + $.08 per mile. Employer is required to pay regular pay in some circumstances. Massachusetts General Laws Annotated, Chapter 262, §25.

Punishment: $2,000 max. fine. M.G.L.A., Ch. 234A, §42.

MICHIGAN

Compensation: Not less than $15 per day + mileage. Michigan Compiled Laws Annotated, §600.1344.

Punishment: $100 max. fine and/or 90 days max. incarceration. M.C.L.A. §730.268.

MINNESOTA

Compensation: Reimbursement for travel, day care, and parking. Minnesota Statutes Annotated, §593.48.

Punishment: Misdemeanor. M.S.A. §593.42.

Mississippi

Compensation: $25 to $40 per day + mileage. Mississippi Code 1972 Annotated, §25-7-61.

Punishment: $100 max. fine and/or 3 days max. incarceration. M.C.A. §13-5-34.

Missouri

Compensation: $6 per day + $.07 per mile. Annotated Missouri Statutes, §494.455.

Punishment: $250 max. fine. A.M.S. §494.450.

Montana

Compensation: $12 per day, until impaneled, then $25 per day; + mileage. Montana Code Annotated, §3-15-201.

Punishment: $50 max. fine. M.C.A. §3-15-321.

Nebraska

Compensation: $35 per day + mileage. Revised Statutes of Nebraska, §33-138.

Punishment: Contempt of court. R.S.N. §25-1611.

NEVADA

Compensation: Jurors in attendance receive $9 per day. Impaneled jurors receive $15 per day for the first 5 days, then $30 per day, + per diem and mileage. Nevada Revised Statutes Annotated, §6.150.

Punishment: $500 max. fine. N.R.S.A. §6.040.

NEW HAMPSHIRE

Compensation: $20 per day + $.20 per mile. New Hampshire Revised Statutes Annotated, §500-A:15.

Punishment: Misdemeanor. N.H.R.S.A. §500-A:20.

NEW JERSEY

Compensation: $5 per day. New Jersey Statutes Annotated, §22A:1-1.1.

Punishment: $500 max. fine or contempt of court. N.J.S.A. §2B:20-14.

NEW MEXICO

Compensation: State minimum wage + mileage. New Mexico Statutes 1978 Annotated, §38-5-15.

Punishment: Misdemeanor. N.M.S.A. §38-5-10.

NEW YORK

Compensation: $40 per day. Some employers (set forth in §519) are prohibited from withholding the first $40 of pay during jury duty, in which case the juror will be paid by the employer and not the state (if paid less than $40 by the employer, the state will make up the difference). Juror will not receive the state compensation if his or her employer pays regular wages during jury service. If juror is required to be present for more than 30 days, an additional $6 per day is paid for each day after 30 days. (**Note:** prior to 2/15/98, the amount was $27.50 per day.) State will also provide food and lodging if necessary, but this will be paid directly to the food vendor or hotel, not to the juror. Consolidated Laws of New York Law, Judiciary Law §521.

Punishment: $250 max. fine. C.L.N.Y., Jud. §527.

NORTH CAROLINA

Compensation: $12 per day for the first 5 days, then $30 per day for more than 5 days within a 24 month period. North Carolina General Statutes, §7A-312.

Punishment: $50 max. fine. N.C.G.S. §9-13.

NORTH DAKOTA

Compensation: $25 per day + mileage at rate paid to state employees. North Dakota Century Code, §27-09.1-14.

Punishment: None in statutes.

OHIO

Compensation: Up to $15 per day for the first 10 days, not less than $15 per day thereafter, + mileage. Ohio Revised Code Annotated, §2313.34.

Punishment: Contempt of court (fine or arrest). O.R.C.A. §§2313.11 and 2313.30.

OKLAHOMA

Compensation: Jurors in attendance receive $12.50 per day, impaneled jurors $20 per day; + mileage. Oklahoma Statutes Annotated, Title 28, §86.

Punishment: None in statutes.

OREGON

Compensation: $10 per day + mileage. Oregon Revised Statutes, §§10.060 and 10.065.

Punishment: Contempt of court, and $300 max. fine. O.R.S. §10.990.

PENNSYLVANIA

Compensation: $9 per day for the first 3 days, then $25 per day; + $.17 per mile. Pennsylvania Consolidated Statutes Annotated, Title 42, §4561.

Punishment: Contempt of court; $500 max. fine and/or 10 days max. incarceration. P.C.S.A., Title 42, §4584.

Rhode Island

Compensation: $15 per day. General Laws of Rhode Island, §9-29-5.

Punishment: Contempt of court; $20 min. fine. G.L.R.I. §9-10-10.

South Carolina

Compensation: $2 to $20 per day, depending on the county; + $.05 to $.10 per mile depending on the county. Code of Laws of South Carolina Code Annotated, §14-7-1370.

Punishment: $20 max. fine. C.L.S.C.A. §14-7-1390.

South Dakota

Compensation: $40 per day + mileage. South Dakota Codified Laws Annotated, §16-13-46.

Punishment: Contempt of court; $5 to $50 fine; after second notice, fine and/or 10 days max. incarceration. S.D.C.L. §16-13-45.

Tennessee

Compensation: $10 per day min.; plus 10¢ per mile or $11 per day. Tennessee Code Annotated, §22-4-101.

Punishment: Contempt of court; $25 max. fine. T.C.A. §22-2-307.

TEXAS

Compensation: $6 to $30 per day, depending on the court. Texas Codes Annotated, Texas Government, §61.001.

Punishment: $10 to $100 fine. T.C.A., Tx. Govt., §62.111.

UTAH

Compensation: $17 per day + mileage if over 50 miles. Utah Code Annotated 1953, §21.5.4.

Punishment: Contempt of court; $100 max. fine and/or 3 days max. incarceration. U.C.A. §78-46-20.

VERMONT

Compensation: $30 per day unless compensated by employer, + per diem. Vermont Statutes Annotated, Title 32, §1511.

Punishment: $50 max. fine. V.S.A., Title 4, §958.

VIRGINIA

Compensation: $30 per day + necessary and reasonable costs. Virginia Code Annotated, §§14.1—195.1.

Punishment: $25 to $100 fine. V.C.A. §§8.01—356.

WASHINGTON

Compensation: $10 to $25 per day, + mileage. Revised Code of Washington Annotated, §2.36.150.

Punishment: Misdemeanor. R.C.W.A. §2.36.170.

West Virginia

Compensation: $15 to $40 per day depending on the court, + mileage at the rate of state employees. West Virginia Code, §52-1-17.

Punishment: Civil contempt of court, $1,000 max. fine. W.V.C. §52-1-24.

Wisconsin

Compensation: At least $16 per day + mileage. Wisconsin Statutes Annotated, §756.25.

Punishment: $40 max. fine. W.S.A. §756.30.

Wyoming

Compensation: $30 per day for first 5 days, then additional $20 per day at discretion of the court. Wyoming Statutes, §1-11-303.

Punishment: Contempt of court, arrest, and being compelled to attend. W.S. §1-11-115.

Notes

Chapter One: Right to Serve

1. 28 U.S.C. Sections 1821, 1861-1869 (1982)

2. *Society of Separationist, Inc. v. Herman,* 939 F.2d 1207 (5th Cir. 1991)

3. *State v. Skaggs,* 586 P.2d 1279 (1978)

4. *Coleman v. United States,* 379 A.2d 951 (1977)

5. *State v. Cashman,* 485 SW2d 431 (1972)

6. *Bobb v. Municipal Court,* 143 Cal. App. 3d 860, 192 Cal. Rptr. 270 (1983)

7. *Texas Employers' Ins. Assoc. v. Brooks,* 414 SW2d 945 (1967)

8. *Commonwealth v. Theberge,* 115 NE 2d 719 (1953)

9. *Commonwealth v. Santiago,* 318 A2d 737 (1974)

10. *Prudencio v. Gonzales,* 727 P2d 553 (1986)

11. *People v. Honeycutt,* 141 Cal Rptr 698, 570 P2d 1050 (1977)

Chapter Two: Right to Compensation

1. *The Uniform Jury Selection and Service Act 1970.*

Chapter Three: Right to Privacy

1. *Whalen v. Roe*, 429 U.S. 589 (1977).

2. *Commonwealth v. Cero*, 264 Mass 264, 162 N.E. 349 (1928).

3. *United States v. Costello*, 255 F.2d 876 (2nd Cir. 1958).

4. *Lehman v. City and County of San Francisco*, 80 Cal App 3d 309, 145 Cal Rptr 493 (1978).

5. *Pointer v. United States*, 151 U.S. 396 (1983).

6. *National Law Journal*, July 3, 1995.

7. *United States v. Sherman*, 581 F.2d 1358 (9th Cir. 1978).

8. *Rakes v. United States*, 169 F.2d 739 (1948).

Chapter Four: Right to Safety

1. *United States v. Bentvena*, 319 F.2d 916 (2nd Cir. 1963).

2. *Remmer v. United States*, 347 U.S. 227 (1954).

3. *United States v. Greer*, 806 F.2d 556 (5th Cir. 1986)

4. *United States v. Zelinka*, 862 F.2d 92 (6th Cir. 1989)

5. *Frankish v. Brookhart*, 877 F.2d 671 (8th Cir. 1989)

6. *United States v. Brodie*, 858 F.2d 492 (9th Cir. 1988)

7. *Dickson v. Sullivan*, 849 F.2d 403 (9th Cir. 1988)

8. *United States v. Edmond*, 730 F.Supp 1144 (1990)

Chapter Five: Right to Nullify

1. *Sparf and Hansen v. United States*, 156 U.S. 51 (1894)

2. *Morisette v. United States*, 342 U.S. 24 (1952)

3. *United States v. Moylan*, 417 F.2d 1006 (4th Cir. 1969)

BIBLIOGRAPHY

Adler, Stephen J., *The Jury: Trial and Error in the American Courtroom*. New York: Times Books, 1994.

Finkel, Norman J., *Commonsense Justice: Juror's Notions of the Law*. Cambridge: Harvard University Press, 1995.

Green, Thomas Andrew, *Verdict According to Conscience*. Chicago: University of Chicago Press, 1985.

Guinther, John, *The Jury in America*. New York: Facts on File Publications, 1988.

Hans, Valerie P., *Judging the Jury*. New York: Plenum Press, 1986.

Hastie, Reid, *Inside the Jury*. Cambridge: Harvard University Press, 1983.

Kassin, Saul M., *The American Jury on Trial*. New York: Hemisphere Pub. Corp., 1988

MacCoun, Robert J., *Experimental Research on Jury Decision-Making*. Santa Monica: Rand Corp., 1989.

Selvin, Molly, *The Debate Over Jury Performance*. Santa Monica: Institute for Civil Justice, Rand, 1987.

Simon, Rita J., *The Jury: Its Role in American Society*. Lexington: D.C. Heath & Co., 1980

INDEX

Your #1 Source for Real World Legal Information...

Sphinx® Publishing
A Division of Sourcebooks, Inc.

- Written by lawyers   • Simple English explanation of the law
- Forms and instructions included

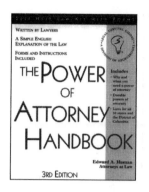

HOW TO MAKE YOUR OWN WILL

Safeguard your family from unnecessary grief by leaving a thorough will. Included are ready-to-use forms and instructions that explain inheritance laws, joint property, pay on death accounts, living wills, and more!

144 pages; $12.95;
ISBN 1-57071-228-X

THE POWER OF ATTORNEY HANDBOOK (2ND EDITION)

It is now easier than ever to authorize someone to act on your behalf for your convenience or necessity. Forms with instructions are included, as well as state-by-state reference guide to power of attorney laws.

140 pages; $19.95;
ISBN 1-57248-044-0

What our customers say about our books:

"It couldn't be more clear for the layperson." —R.D.

"I want you to know I really appreciate your book. It has saved me a lot of time and money." —L.T.

"Your real estate contracts book has saved me nearly $12,000.00 in closing costs over the past year." —A.B.

"...many of the legal questions that I have had over the years were answered clearly and concisely through your plain English interpretation of the law." —C.E.H.

"If there weren't people out there like you I'd be lost. You have the best books of this type out there." —S.B.

"...your forms and directions are easy to follow." —C.V.M.

Sphinx® Publishing's Legal Survival Guides are directly available from the publisher, or from your local bookstores.

*For credit card orders call 1–800–43–BRIGHT,
write P.O. Box 372, Naperville, IL 60566, or fax 630-961-2168*

Sphinx® Publishing's State Titles
Up-to-date for Your State

California

CA Power of Attorney Handbook	$12.95
How to File for Divorce in CA	$19.95
How to Make a CA Will	$12.95
How to Probate an Estate in CA	$19.95
How to Start a Business in CA	$16.95
How to Win in Small Claims Court in CA	$14.95
Landlords' Rights and Duties in CA	$19.95

Florida

Florida Power of Attorney Handbook (2E)	$12.95
How to File for Divorce in FL (5E)	$21.95
How to Form a Partnership in FL	$19.95
How to Form a Nonprofit Corp in FL (3E)	$19.95
How to Form a Corporation in FL (4E)	$19.95
How to Make a FL Will (5E)	$12.95
How to Modify Your FL Divorce Judgement (3E)	$22.95
How to Probate an Estate in FL (3E)	$24.95
How to Start a Business in FL (4E)	$16.95
How to Win in Small Claims Court in FL (6E)	$14.95
Landlords' Rights and Duties in FL (7E)	$19.95
Land Trusts in FL (5E)	$24.95
Women's Legal Rights in FL	$19.95

Georgia

How to File for Divorce in GA (3E)	$19.95
How to Make a GA Will (2E)	$9.95
How to Start and Run a GA Business (2E)	$18.95

Illinois

How to File for Divorce in IL (2E)	$19.95
How to Make an IL Will (2E)	$12.95
How to Start a Business in IL (2E)	$16.95

Massachusetts

How to File for Divorce in MA (2E)	$19.95
How to Make a MA Will	$9.95
How to Probate an Estate in MA	$19.95
How to Start a Business in MA	$16.95
Landlords' Rights and Duties in MA	$19.95

Sphinx® Publishing's Legal Survival Guides are directly available from the publisher, or from your local bookstores.

MICHIGAN

How to File for Divorce in MI (2E)	$19.95
How to Make a MI Will	$9.95
How to Start a Business in MI (2E)	$16.95

MINNESOTA

How to File for Divorce in MN	$19.95
How to Form a Simple Corporation in MN	$19.95
How to Make a MN Will	$9.95
How to Start a Business in MN	$16.95

NEW YORK

How to File for Divorce in NY	$19.95
How to Make a NY Will	$12.95
How to Start a Business in NY	$16.95
How to Win in Small Claims Court in NY	$14.95
Landlords' Rights and Duties in NY	$19.95
New York Power of Attorney Handbook	$19.95

NORTH CAROLINA

How to File for Divorce in NC (2E)	$19.95
How to Make a NC Will (2E)	$12.95
How to Start a Business in NC	$16.95

PENNSYLVANIA

How to File for Divorce in PA	$19.95
How to Make a PA Will	$12.95
How to Start a Business in PA	$16.95
Landlords' Rights and Duties in PA	$19.95

TEXAS

How to File for Divorce in TX (2E)	$19.95
How to Form a Simple Corporation in TX	$19.95
How to Make a TX Will (2E)	$12.95
How to Probate an Estate in TX	$19.95
How to Start a Business in TX (2E)	$16.95
How to Win in Small Claims Court in TX	$14.95
Landlords' Rights and Duties in TX	$19.95

For credit card orders call 1–800–43–BRIGHT,
write P.O. Box 372, Naperville, IL 60566, or fax 630-961-2168

Sphinx® Publishing's National Titles
Valid in All 50 States

Legal Survival in Business

How to Form Your Own Corporation (2E)	$19.95
How to Form Your Own Partnership	$19.95
How to Register Your Own Copyright (2E)	$19.95
How to Register Your Own Trademark (2E)	$19.95
Most Valuable Business Legal Forms You'll Ever Need (2E)	$19.95
Most Valuable Corporate Forms You'll Ever Need (2E)	$24.95
Software Law (with diskette)	$29.95

Legal Survival in Court

Crime Victim's Guide to Justice	$19.95
Debtors' Rights (3E)	$12.95
Defend Yourself against Criminal Charges	$19.95
Grandparents' Rights	$19.95
Help Your Lawyer Win Your Case	$12.95
How to Win Your Unemployment Compensation Claim	$19.95
Jurors' Rights (2E)	$9.95
Legal Malpractice and Other Claims against Your Lawyer	$18.95
Legal Research Made Easy	$14.95
Simple Ways to Protect Yourself from Lawsuits	$24.95
Victim's Rights	$12.95
Winning Your Personal Injury Claim	$19.95

Legal Survival in Real Estate

How to Buy a Condominium or Townhome	$16.95
How to Negotiate Real Estate Contracts (3E)	$16.95
How to Negotiate Real Estate Leases (3E)	$16.95
Successful Real Estate Brokerage Management	$19.95

Legal Survival in Personal Affairs

How to File Your Own Bankruptcy (4E)	$19.95
How to File Your Own Divorce (3E)	$19.95
How to Make Your Own Will	$12.95
How to Write Your Own Living Will	$9.95
How to Write Your Own Premarital Agreement (2E)	$19.95
How to Win Your Unemployment Compensation Claim	$19.95
Living Trusts and Simple Ways to Avoid Probate (2E)	$19.95
Most Valuable Personal Legal Forms You'll Ever Need	$14.95
Neighbor vs. Neighbor	$12.95
The Power of Attorney Handbook (3E)	$19.95
Simple Ways to Protect Yourself from Lawsuits	$24.95
Social Security Benefits Handbook (2E)	$14.95
Unmarried Parents' Rights	$19.95
U.S.A. Immigration Guide (3E)	$19.95
Guia de Inmigracion a Estados Unidos	$19.95

SPHINX® PUBLISHING ORDER FORM

<table>
<tr><td>BILL TO:</td><td>SHIP TO:</td></tr>
</table>

Phone #	Terms	F.O.B.	Chicago, IL	Ship Date

Charge my: ☐ VISA ☐ MasterCard ☐ American Express ☐ **Money Order or Personal Check**

Credit Card Number   **Expiration Date**

Qty	ISBN	Title	Retail	Qty	ISBN	Title	Retail
		SPHINX PUBLISHING'S NATIONAL TITLES			1-57071-348-0	The Power of Attorney Handbook (3E)	$19.95
	1-57071-166-6	Crime Victim's Guide to Justice	$19.95		1-57248-020-3	Simple Ways to Protect Yourself from Lawsuits	$24.95
	1-57071-342-1	Debtors' Rights (3E)	$12.95		1-57071-337-5	Social Security Benefits Handbook (2E)	$14.95
	1-57071-162-3	Defend Yourself Against Criminal Charges	$19.95		1-57071-163-1	Software Law (w/diskette)	$29.95
	1-57248-001-7	Grandparents' Rights	$19.95		0-913825-86-7	Successful Real Estate Brokerage Mgmt.	$19.95
	0-913825-99-9	Guia de Inmigracion a Estados Unidos	$19.95		1-57071-399-5	Unmarried Parents' Rights	$19.95
	1-57248-021-1	Help Your Lawyer Win Your Case	$12.95		1-57071-354-5	U.S.A. Immigration Guide (3E)	$19.95
	1-57071-164-X	How to Buy a Condominium or Townhome	$16.95		0-913825-82-4	Victims' Rights	$12.95
	1-57071-223-9	How to File Your Own Bankruptcy (4E)	$19.95		1-57071-165-8	Winning Your Personal Injury Claim	$19.95
	1-57071-224-7	How to File Your Own Divorce (3E)	$19.95			**CALIFORNIA TITLES**	
	1-57071-227-1	How to Form Your Own Corporation (2E)	$19.95		1-57071-360-X	CA Power of Attorney Handbook	$12.95
	1-57071-343-X	How to Form Your Own Partnership	$19.95		1-57071-355-3	How to File for Divorce in CA	$19.95
	1-57071-228-X	How to Make Your Own Will	$12.95		1-57071-356-1	How to Make a CA Will	$12.95
	1-57071-331-6	How to Negotiate Real Estate Contracts (3E)	$16.95		1-57071-408-8	How to Probate an Estate in CA	$19.95
	1-57071-332-4	How to Negotiate Real Estate Leases (3E)	$16.95		1-57071-357-X	How to Start a Business in CA	$16.95
	1-57071-225-5	How to Register Your Own Copyright (2E)	$19.95		1-57071-358-8	How to Win in Small Claims Court in CA	$14.95
	1-57071-226-3	How to Register Your Own Trademark (2E)	$19.95		1-57071-359-6	Landlords' Rights and Duties in CA	$19.95
	1-57071-349-9	How to Win Your Unemployment Compensation Claim	$19.95			**FLORIDA TITLES**	
	1-57071-167-4	How to Write Your Own Living Will	$9.95		1-57071-363-4	Florida Power of Attorney Handbook (2E)	$9.95
	1-57071-344-8	How to Write Your Own Premarital Agreement (2E)	$19.95		1-57071-403-7	How to File for Divorce in FL (5E)	$21.95
	1-57071-333-2	Jurors' Rights (2E)	$9.95		1-57071-401-0	How to Form a Partnership in FL	$19.95
	1-57248-032-7	Legal Malpractice and Other Claims Against...	$18.95		1-57248-004-1	How to Form a Nonprofit Corp. in FL (3E)	$19.95
	1-57248-008-4	Legal Research Made Easy	$14.95		1-57071-380-4	How to Form a Corporation in FL (4E)	$19.95
	1-57071-336-7	Living Trusts and Simple Ways to Avoid Probate (2E)	$19.95		1-57071-361-8	How to Make a FL Will (5E)	$12.95
	1-57071-345-6	Most Valuable Bus. Legal Forms You'll Ever Need (2E)	$19.95		1-57248-056-4	How to Modify Your FL Divorce Judgement (3E)	$22.95
	1-57071-346-4	Most Valuable Corporate Forms You'll Ever Need (2E)	$24.95		1-57071-364-2	How to Probate an Estate in FL (3E)	$24.95
	1-57071-347-2	Most Valuable Personal Legal Forms You'll Ever Need	$14.95				
	0-913825-41-7	Neighbor vs. Neighbor	$12.95			***Form Continued on Following Page*** **SUBTOTAL** _____	

Qty	ISBN	Title	Retail
		FLORIDA TITLES (CONT'D)	
_____	1-57248-005-X	How to Start a Business in FL (4E)	$16.95
_____	1-57071-362-6	How to Win in Small Claims Court in FL (6E)	$14.95
_____	1-57071-335-9	Landlords' Rights and Duties in FL (7E)	$19.95
_____	1-57071-334-0	Land Trusts in FL (5E)	$24.95
_____	0-913825-73-5	Women's Legal Rights in FL	$19.95
		GEORGIA TITLES	
_____	1-57071-376-6	How to File for Divorce in GA (3E)	$19.95
_____	1-57248-047-5	How to Make a GA Will (2E)	$9.95
_____	1-57248-026-2	How to Start and Run a GA Business (2E)	$18.95
		ILLINOIS TITLES	
_____	1-57071-405-3	How to File for Divorce in IL (2E)	$19.95
_____	1-57071-415-0	How to Make an IL Will (2E)	$12.95
_____	1-57071-416-9	How to Start a Business in IL (2E)	$16.95
		MASSACHUSETTS TITLES	
_____	1-57071-329-4	How to File for Divorce in MA (2E)	$19.95
_____	1-57248-050-5	How to Make a MA Will	$9.95
_____	1-57248-053-X	How to Probate an Estate in MA	$19.95
_____	1-57248-054-8	How to Start a Business in MA	$16.95
_____	1-57248-055-6	Landlords' Rights and Duties in MA	$19.95
		MICHIGAN TITLES	
_____	1-57071-409-6	How to File for Divorce in MI (2E)	$19.95
_____	1-57248-015-7	How to Make a MI Will	$9.95
_____	1-57071-407-X	How to Start a Business in MI (2E)	$16.95
		MINNESOTA TITLES	
_____	1-57248-039-4	How to File for Divorce in MN	$19.95
_____	1-57248-040-8	How to Form a Simple Corporation in MN	$19.95
_____	1-57248-037-8	How to Make a MN Will	$9.95
_____	1-57248-038-6	How to Start a Business in MN	$16.95
		NEW YORK TITLES	
_____	1-57071-184-4	How to File for Divorce in NY	$19.95
_____	1-57071-183-6	How to Make a NY Will	$12.95

Qty	ISBN	Title	Retail
_____	1-57071-185-2	How to Start a Business in NY	$16.95
_____	1-57071-187-9	How to Win in Small Claims Court in NY	$14.95
_____	1-57071-186-0	Landlords' Rights and Duties in NY	$19.95
_____	1-57071-188-7	New York Power of Attorney Handbook	$19.95
		NORTH CAROLINA TITLES	
_____	1-57071-326-X	How to File for Divorce in NC (2E)	$19.95
_____	1-57071-327-8	How to Make a NC Will (2E)	$12.95
_____	0-913825-93-X	How to Start a Business in NC	$16.95
		PENNSYLVANIA TITLES	
_____	1-57071-177-1	How to File for Divorce in PA	$19.95
_____	1-57071-176-3	How to Make a PA Will	$12.95
_____	1-57071-178-X	How to Start a Business in PA	$16.95
_____	1-57071-179-8	Landlords' Rights and Duties in PA	$19.95
		TEXAS TITLES	
_____	1-57071-330-8	How to File for Divorce in TX (2E)	$19.95
_____	1-57248-009-2	How to Form a Simple Corporation in TX	$19.95
_____	1-57071-417-7	How to Make a TX Will (2E)	$12.95
_____	1-57071-418-5	How to Probate an Estate in TX (2E)	$19.95
_____	1-57071-365-0	How to Start a Business in TX (2E)	$16.95
_____	1-57248-012-2	How to Win in Small Claims Court in TX	$14.95
_____	1-57248-011-4	Landlords' Rights and Duties in TX	$19.95

SUBTOTAL THIS SIDE _____

SUBTOTAL OTHER SIDE _____

Illinois residents add 6.75% sales tax Florida residents add 6% state sales tax plus applicable discretionary surtax _____

Shipping— $4.00 for 1st book, $1.00 each additional _____

TOTAL _____